PRAISE FOR *LEGITIMATE KID*

"Rodriguez . . . brings heart and humor to universal issues such as race, motherhood, and survival, often through the lens of Latinx experiences."
—*Los Angeles Times*

"Aida Rodriguez is part of the next wave of talented comedic storytellers that I dreamed about when I was trying to break down barriers in the industry. Besides being a fierce Latina powerhouse, she's FUNNY AS HELL! So buy this book. No really, BUY THIS BOOK!!! I don't want any problems, ya heard?!"
—John Leguizamo, Emmy and Tony Award–winning actor, writer, and producer

"Funny doesn't come easy. Sometimes funny comes from humiliation, heartbreak, and a lifetime of hard knocks. Sometimes it rises like a phoenix from the ashes. *Legitimate Kid* is a tribute to Aida's comedic art—to her ability to dig down, bring up the pain, and transform it magically, mercifully into stories that lighten the load. This is a book that confronts not only the question of 'illegitimate' birth, but also the larger question of social legitimacy, of one's place in a heartless caste system, of the business of being a Latina. It will stay with you for a very long time."
—Marie Arana, author of *American Chica*; *Bolívar*; *Silver, Sword, and Stone*; and *LatinoLand*

"*Legitimate Kid* is a significant book for the culture. It speaks to those in society who feel ostracized and marginalized by America's institutions that are designed to maintain the status quo. The book demonstrates how Aida evolved into a frontline warrior in the fight to legitimize and raise the value of African Americans, Latino Americans, and Afro-Latino Americans. She speaks truth in such a transparent and courageous way about the challenges within her community and the importance of holding ▒▒▒ ▒▒▒▒ ▒▒▒▒ ▒▒▒ ▒▒▒ ▒▒▒ ▒king us laugh along the way. I know, this memoir."
—Ben Crump ▒▒▒ *Open Season*

"Aida's journey will ins▒▒ ▒▒▒ oals but your fears. What a delight it ▒▒▒ *te Kid*."
—Julissa Arce, author of *You Sound Like a White Girl*

Legit

imate

A MEMOIR

Kid

AIDA RODRIGUEZ

FOREWORD BY ARIANA DeBOSE

HarperOne
An Imprint of HarperCollins*Publishers*

HarperCollins books may be purchased for educational, business, or sales promotional use. For information, please email the Special Markets Department at SPsales@harpercollins.com.

FIRST HARPERCOLLINS PAPERBACK PUBLISHED IN 2024

Designed by Elina Cohen

Library of Congress Cataloging-in-Publication Data is available upon request.

ISBN 978-0-06-324129-9

24 25 26 27 28 LBC 5 4 3 2 1

All praises to the Most High, the Saints, the Angels, and the Ancestors. I am thankful for your guidance, protection, and love.

Omar and Akaylah,

Thank you for being my WHY when I didn't feel like I was enough. I am so honored to be a part of our holy trinity. I will be by your side until the end and then I will haunt you after. I have received no greater love than that you have given me, love you back, more and then some.

Mami,

This book is a testament to your strength, love, and growth. It took me becoming a mother to understand everything you gave so that I could be. What I counted as a mistake as your child, I learned to process as human error as a mother. You will always be the Queen of my Universe. Thank you for every sacrifice.

David/China, Carlos/Istata, and Jasmin/Pachew,

I would do it over again, if I got to do it with you. I love you unconditionally and infinitely.

Aida/Abuela,

Te adoro para siempre. Bendición.

Carlos, Raymond, Pedro, Richard, and David,

After believing for so long that I did not have a father, I woke up one day knowing that each of you was just that. My powerful five, thank you.

One cannot consent to creep when one feels an impulse to soar.

—Helen Keller

A la la la la la la . . . que cante mi gente.

—Johnny Pacheco, as sung by Héctor Lavoe

CONTENTS

PART I:

Cocoon

PART II:

Metamorphosis

PART III:

Wings

PART IV:

Flight

FOREWORD

I am so glad you're here.

Before I properly lead you through why I think this book is important, why I believe it will resonate with you, and how I hope it might rewire, or at the very least impact, your thinking, let me tell you a story.

In early 2019, an announcement was broadcast through various media outlets that famed director Steven Spielberg had cast an actress in the role of Anita in his much-anticipated film, *West Side Story*. That actress was Afro-Latina, she was queer, and she was *me*. Ultimately there was a lot of excitement, which was thrilling to experience, but there was also a fair share of negativity. There is always an equal axiiind opposite reaction, right? And some of those negative comments were echoing what was already happening in my head: "She's not Latina enough. She doesn't even speak Spanish. Who is she?!" While I was struggling with all these questions of legitimacy, it was like the universe sent me an angel from heaven in the form of a brilliant Latina comedian, Aida Rodriguez (whom, I would like to add, I had already been following for QUITE some time. Yes, I was a fan!).

In true 2019 fashion, Aida DMed me on Instagram: "We got you." I felt buoyed by her simple, empowering message; and it reminded me of who I was and what I knew I could do. When *WSS* was released, Aida bought out a theater in Los Angeles and filled it with Latinos, Afro-Latinos, and Black people . . . everyone from our underrepresented communities was invited and included. With these acts of support, both large and small, a relationship was born with a human I am so in awe of, and so inspired by. I truly can't believe I get to call Aida my friend. If she can do that for me with one simple text, just imagine what she can do for you with this memoir.

Point of order, this is truly a MEMOIR. There are surely laughs along the way, it's Aida, after all . . . but it's not all lighthearted content. While being both direct and circuitous, straightforward and veiled, revealing and protective, she guides her reader through an unflinching look at her past, her community, and her culture. She holds the mirror up to everything and tells you what she sees with truthful enthusiasm and a form of honesty that is rare when talking about identity politics as they pertain to the individual and the community at large. The finest comedians are the ones who can share this level of transparency yet find humor in their struggles. They extract hilarity from pain. Aida is one of the finest comedians and I personally think she's the best of us.

Although Aida and I frequently texted, DMed, and spoke on the phone, the first time I met my modern pen pal in person was when I went to see her perform in early 2022. She was the headliner at Caroline's, a historic landmark institution for comedy in New York City. I was so stoked to be able to see her in action, I brought my whole queer family with me to support her. Not only was she at the top of her game that night, but what really got me was her attention to the details. For instance, Aida made sure every performer she shared the stage with that night was Latine, which within the comedy space, takes intention. The Aida you see in her comedy specials or on TV and the Aida I connected with over the phone are truly the Aida you get in person. It's a rarity, but with her what you see is what you get. They say to never meet your heroes, but I say always meet Aida Rodriguez.

In this book Aida speaks eloquently and thoughtfully about her search for legitimacy, something I was searching for early on in life and, at times, still am. I've had firsthand experience with being ostracized from the communities that are wholeheartedly a part of my DNA. Remember the *West Side Story* casting announcement? That's just one example. And I could pontificate further but I don't have to, because in this memoir Aida puts pen to paper to describe the very feelings I've held around the search for legitimacy within the communities I belong to. Aida examines what it means to seek legitimacy as a woman, as a Latina, as a daughter, a mother, and simply as a human being.

Much of Aida's comedy is based on race relations and on her experiences in the Latine community, but it's also universally human. She's not afraid to tackle how our communities self-police, how we judge and decide who gets to do and be what. Who's accepted and who's rejected. So often we operate from a scarcity mindset—there aren't enough roles for everyone, there's only one seat at the table for a person of color. Aida is the antithesis of that. She's wildly generous. She's on her path. She's doing the work and pursuing her dreams and she's bringing everyone along with her. She makes difficult conversations tangible, finding common ground among us all.

This book is a beautiful example of how you can acknowledge your culture and your community, and take accountability for your role within it. This is not a book about blame, it's about truth. She holds herself accountable for her decisions and the narratives she's told herself about herself that aren't true. She critically examines her choices along her path as she navigates a professional world dominated by men, and mostly white men, and is honest about her successes as well as her missteps.

When you blaze a challenging trail and your path through life isn't easy, it can be so simple to have a permanent chip on your shoulder and to blame others for your own challenges. Aida and I connected so quickly and profoundly because we operate from a similar mindset: do good things, do good work, and put good energy out into the world. You might not always receive that same goodness back, but when you do, you know you've earned it.

What an act of defiance to tell your own story instead of letting others do it for you. What an audacious achievement to know you can contain contradictory multitudes. You can be proud of your *culture* and know that we still have things to fix. You can be proud of your *community* and still call out problematic patterns and structures. You can be proud of yourself and still know you have work to do. After all, Aida will let a bitch know what the shit is.

I adore Aida Rodriguez. I adore this book, and reading it, I've never felt more seen. And I hope you do too.

Ariana DeBose

INTRODUCTION

I am so happy that you are here, thank you for taking this trip with me. This is the note I write when I sign copies of my memoir. October 17, 2023, will always be one of the most important days of my life. It was the day the realization that I had actually written a book hit me, like my mother's belt when I was a kid. I can't tell you how much joy I have experienced in the last few months—the events, book fairs, and meet-and-greets—while coming face-to-face with reflections of myself and my journey in all corners of the country.

Writing this book didn't start off as a joyful experience. When I first embarked on the journey of putting my life into words, I didn't believe I was capable. My body grew soar and stiff, my hands shook with angst, and my spirit was low. I had been through so many things in life and had accepted that good things were not on the menu for me; I wasn't worthy. I didn't know how I was going to come up with eighty thousand words that would sum up my life.

As I sat down to write *Legitimate Kid*, I had to go back to the beginning and ask myself "Why?" Is this for fame and accolades? Is this to be on bestseller lists? To elevate my career as a comedian, an actor? As a resounding "Hell no!" rang loudly in my head, I remember laughing to myself.

One morning I sat on the beach, thinking of all the people I remembered from the block where I grew up. All those faces that meant everything to me, yet meant nothing to anyone outside our little corner of the world. I thought about my great-grandfather, Sixto; my grandmother, Aida; my uncles, Carlos and Raymond, who had transitioned; and my father, who had always been a ghost in my life. And then my mother, the one person I had always believed I could save. My children 'Omar and Akaylah came up, the ones who saved me. Through them, I learned a love I never thought possible. Things began to change for me, and I started to feel some kind of clarity. Then I thought about meeting with my father for my HBO comedy special, *Fighting Words*, and how I wanted to write about it, but comedy wasn't working. It was hard to laugh at a wound not yet healed. Writing became the only way through. My whole life, I had been searching for legitimacy, and these pages would grant it to me.

As I continue to heal the little girl within, here I am now, renewing this commitment. I am forever humbled by the hugs, the tears, the birth certificates, and most importantly, the connection to a network of survivors who took on my words as validation. I hope you know that you came here "legitimate," and no one can grant that to you or take it away. I hope my book inspires you to remember the quiet ones, the ones who showed up, and the ones who loved you just because, and that you are reminded of who we are when we are stripped of the titles and constructs that limit us in our humanity. And most importantly, I hope you walk away from this trip declaring your own legitimacy and unleashing it onto this world with reckless abandon.

PART I

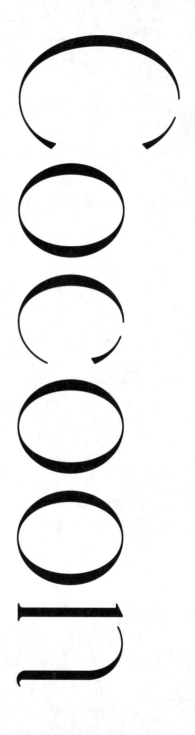

Legitimacy

When I was twelve, I asked my mom why I had her last name and why she wasn't married. I had been thinking about it for the past four years, but I wasn't brave enough to bring it up. My awareness as a kid was advanced, I was exposed to so much. I was a translator, an assistant, a babysitter, and everything and anything else that was needed. Because of the things I had heard the adults talk about, I sensed that there was some shame surrounding the issue. The last thing I ever wanted was to make my mother feel bad. She was young and had been through a lot—and I had witnessed much of it firsthand.

But the truth is that, until I became a stand-up comedian, I didn't like to say my name. It's simple: I did not have my father's last name and I was ashamed of it. I didn't always feel that way, nor was I even aware of this, until the third grade. I was an "innocent," minding my own business, when one day a rotten kid in my class named Beth called me a "bastard." Though I didn't know what that meant, I was pretty sure it wasn't nice, because nothing good could come from this kid. Beth was the first child that I'd describe as evil. She was always making fun of other kids and was extremely mean. It was as if she felt joy in making others feel bad.

I remember the other children who sat at our table laughing at Beth's comment. They were just relieved that the heat wasn't on them since this spawn of Satan would unleash her wrath on any of us at any time. All the kids laughed and taunted me, except for Alvaro, my cute, chubby Cuban buddy. He had the thickest lisp and the most animated way of telling utterly depressing stories. Even when he told us that his dog died, he painted a colorful scene of how a car hit his puppy. "Whoosh!" he said, as his two hands collided, stopping for effect before concluding, "And poof, no more puppy." It was hard not to laugh, but I didn't. He had an accent and speech impediment and I knew laughing would make him feel bad.

Thinking about other peoples' feelings before my own made me terrible at the dozens. The dozens was a game we played in our neighborhoods, a game of shame. We'd make fun of each other for street cred. There were many different names for it: cracking, roasting, and so on. It was very personal; nothing was off limits. It was a defense mechanism to keep everyone off of you and the terrible things that were happening in your own life. I had already developed a sense of shame, I wasn't going to step out and be vulnerable to being called out on some of the awful shit about my life. I had no presence; I was too mousy—definitely not the signs of a future comedian.

But Alvaro was also kind, and he responded in my defense, "No, she's not a bastard!" I am sure he didn't know what the word meant either, since he barely knew English. Still, it was as though someone saw me at that moment and knew that I was feeling naked. Alvaro knew what it felt like to be the butt of a joke and if he couldn't save himself from one, he would at least stand up to those horrible fucking kids for me. I tried to be the best friend that I could to him, picking up his lunch box when someone would knock it down. Anything I could do to help. It made me so mad because if the other kids would've taken the time to get to know him, they would've discovered how nice he was and how funny he could be. But the two of us didn't stand a chance against Beth and her posse. They outnumbered us and they were trash-ass kids. Through it all, though, Alvaro had my back.

Loyalty was valued where I grew up—sometimes your survival depended on who was on your team, who would show up for you. As a kid, I can't remember many friends who stood up for me. Yet, here I am, remembering Alvaro so clearly, it meant the world at the time.

All the same, Beth continued, "Your daddy didn't sign your birth certificate!" The bad seed kept laughing in my face. She had been watching me closely and had overheard Mrs. Flannagan talking to my mom. She kept hearing the teacher call my mom Ms. Rodriguez and deduced that my father was not in my life. Guessing that my mom was probably not married either, she took that and ran with it. I couldn't dispute it because it was true and far from uncommon in my neighborhood. Funny thing is that even though Beth had her father's last name, that sucker was not around either. But that didn't stop her from holding that last name thing over me.

It was a tough day, coupled with me wearing Payless Pro Wings and those cheap Wrangler jeans that were too short for me. This was all material for the dozens; unfortunately for me, that muscle would not develop until I turned twelve and finally developed a voice, a funny one. It happened during a bus ride home and, quite honestly, I was fed up with being made fun of for being tall, so I fought back. A boy named Allen, who sat in the back and made fun of everyone, caught me on the wrong day. He was very short and constantly ragged on the taller girls. This day it was my turn. I had enough of being called the Jolly Green Giant.

"Shut up or I'm going to tell the cops you ride around without your car seat."

All the kids broke out in laughter. To this day, I don't know if it was actually that funny, but he shut his little ass up for the rest of the ride. That was the day I was invited to sit in the back of the bus.

But until then, I quietly took it all, and on that day in third grade, Beth just wouldn't let up—she made that year impossible. All I wanted was to get home. In fact, my only greater wish was that I could blink and it would be Friday so the week could be over already. When something shitty like Beth happened at school, I expected to go home so Mom could make it all better. But nope, she made it worse. I asked her what a bastard was and she responded in the most cavalier manner, "It's an illegitimate kid. It means you don't have your father's last name." My world was crushed! In my mother's defense, she had only heard this as a common and casual term, and had too many other things to worry about at the time to think about how that definition could affect me.

My mom was living under my grandmother's roof and rule and desperately wanted to break out. But she didn't have the financial independence to do so. She hadn't finished school and couldn't afford a sitter outside of the family, but trying to be my mother and seeking another way out became her mission.

I was just eight years old when I became conscious of the absence of my father in a real way—Beth made sure of it. What really started to shape my definition of fatherhood was watching the few kids I knew interact with their fathers. Based on my observations, a father was a protector, an uplifter—the man you call Daddy and he calls you his princess in return. The more I delved into it, the more I started to define what not having a father meant for me: My life was going to be fucked. Anybody and everybody would be able to do anything to me because the man who was supposed to stand up for me in this world was not there to protect me. I believed it was only going to be my mom and me—no daddy in or out of the house. I saw myself as vulnerable to the world because a dad meant security and safety. Beth reminded me that I was different and less than. Me not having his last name was just a mark to let others know that I was a target, that I was of lesser value and importance than the kids who were "legitimate." They were better than me and that was how it was going to always be. I couldn't articulate it quite this way at that age, but I definitely know now that was how it felt.

Why didn't I have another last name like the other kids at school whose moms are not with the dads? I had the same last name as my mother, grandmother, and five uncles and I just didn't understand why. My friend Rosie Montez had her father's last name and her mom was broke and single just like mine. I investigated, I wanted to know. I was gathering the strength to ask, although, honestly, I didn't know if this was one of those things that would get me in trouble. I spent many years observing other kids and their situations, grade after grade, until I finally decided to do it.

"Why am I a Rodriguez?" I asked my mother one day when I was twelve years old. I had been heavy with this thought since the third grade. Family origin was something that poor kids in my neighborhood would leverage to assess one another's worth. Many of us didn't have our biological fathers and were receiving state assistance. So the "at least I have my daddy's last name" meant "at least I'm not you, the kid whose father was so bad that he didn't even bother to let the world know you were his."

From that point on, I focused on my first name, even if I allowed everyone to mispronounce it. My first name had a story. Aside from it being one of the most celebrated operas and musicals about a princess and having a rich history during the Matriarch times in Ethiopia, it was also the name of both of my grandmothers. Isn't that something? Two women from two different countries—Puerto Rico and the Dominican Republic—who never met had the same damn name. I didn't know one of those Aidas, my father's mother. I grew up with the other. She was my best friend and I was proud to be her namesake. She was the one who took care of my mother and me and was such a strong lady. She filled in the blanks left by my dad's absence.

It turns out that my dad was in fact present when I was born. According to my grandma, he was in the delivery room in Brigham Young Women's Hospital in Boston, pacing and doing all the dad stuff. She told me how happy and proud he was that day. Yet, all I could think about was why he didn't grab a pen and sign my birth certificate. What was it that held him back? Did he not want me? Did he think I wasn't his? My grandmother said he threw the biggest party to celebrate my birth and baptism. It was my mother's mother who was gushing about it being the proudest moment in his life. He was a beaming father. So why not slap his government on that piece of paper then?

My grandmother went on and on about how much he loved me, so much so, that he insisted on taking us back to his country, the Dominican Republic. He couldn't stand to be without me, she would tell me. That was a good story to grow up with, something positive to feel about him in his absence. But the reality was that he had been deported and he had to go back; it wasn't some romantic trip. Still, she said he wouldn't leave me, and that made me feel good. My grandmother was always one to build me up, constantly pouring into me. She reminded me that I was perfect just the way I was and that everyone in my life was lucky to have me.

My father had been deported more than once. And this time the government meant business: either take your ass home or get ready to make license plates. My family tried to use my birth as a method to keep him in the United States, but that didn't work. Maybe he should've signed my birth certificate. Life in the States could have been better for all of us; there were more opportunities than in the Dominican Republic. Yet he thought that we would go to his country and things would change for the better, and that it would be okay, because he would be back home with his family. He must've really believed this because staying in the States was not an option.

Escaping from home, where she was being sexually abused by a relative, my teenage mom up and left Boston and moved to the Dominican Republic, where she knew no one, to start a life with this man, who was twelve years her senior. She had had it bad at home and just wanted out—I can understand that now. When she met him, he swept her off her feet, and she immediately fell in love. He was charismatic and loving and, most important, he never laid a hand on her. Her bar was there, and though I want to judge it, I can't. We have all had our own toxic relationships, she was just a kid, she deserves a pass.

As the story goes, when she first laid eyes on him at her fifteenth birthday party, she claims he was the most beautiful man she had ever seen. All the while, what jumped out at me in her telling of how they'd first met was the word *man*. Who looks at a grown-ass man in their teens and says, "I want to be with him." That sounded so gross to me, but I kept it to myself. She was feeling all the goods as she shared her love story with me and I didn't want to ruin the moment for her, even though as a kid, it all just sounded super confusing, like stuff that wasn't supposed to happen. Yet there I was, ingesting all my parent's traumas—they were becoming a part of me. This man was a whole-ass grown-up dating a little girl who was running away from home. Her body and brain were not even fully developed, but the smile on her face as she shared this story with me said it all. She had really been into that man. These few positive stories involving my father fueled my desire to find and meet him, even if I was aware of some of the bad stuff that went down.

When we got to Santo Domingo our world was turned upside down. My mom couldn't get her bearings, emotionally, financially, and socially. I don't remember meeting my paternal grandmother, but she wasn't very welcoming—at least, that's what my mother told me. There were also some cultural clashes that caused dissent. My mother is a Puerto Rican, an Indigenous woman, and that was not flying in my father's side of the family. I still don't understand how this could be an issue, but Latinos' thinking has been colonized as well, so we do dumb shit to one another. We find reasons to dislike one another and attach values to our worth based on what white supremacy dictates. To me it was like a figurative mangú, los tres golpes (the three hits): machismo, colorism, and ignorance. Yeah, I would've preferred the fried cheese.

According to my mother, my father—the merengue singer—had a "ho problem." He was popular with the ladies. In fact, when she met him back in Boston, he was linked to several other women. She said that he made her feel like the others were after him, but he chose her, and she was the special one. All the while he was still messing around with other women and that was cause for my mom to have several fights in the neighborhood. She had the fuel for that. When she met my dad, all the anger she stored up from being victimized at home and losing her first baby could be dispensed at any moment, on command.

While we were in the Dominican Republic, my father spent a lot of the time on the road and would leave us with his mother. The only problem was that his mother did not like my mother. My mom was a fighter and not afraid to speak up for herself at this point. What did she have to lose? Legend has it that the other Aida was a terrible bully. My grandmother didn't appreciate my mother not submitting to her will. She really thought she was going to add my mom to the roster of people who followed her directions and tolerated her bullshit. My father's sister, who was also very young, was mousy and tender; my mother was the complete opposite. So when my dad would go off to play his gigs and binge with his bitches, we were left at this woman's mercy. That meant sometimes sleeping outside, sometimes not eating, oftentimes getting bitten by giant mosquitoes. Eventually, my mother couldn't take it anymore, and we left, never to return. I don't even have a single memory of the relatives I left behind and my life there. My paternal brother told me that my grandmother had a reputation for being a tough ass.

After our return to the States the memory of my father faded. He wasn't like the deadbeat parents who make the occasional visit and fill you with false expectations and disappoint you from time to time about picking you up. I never saw him again. I had no information on his whereabouts and knew nothing about him other than the morsels of information my grandmother would feed me to put me at ease. He was totally off limits with my mother, Margarita. I just knew to never bring him up.

Although I was wounded by his absence, it pushed me to become a better person in some ways. In fact, I worked hard to be a "good kid." I did well in school. I was actually a teacher pleaser. In my view, educators were the ones who held my fate in their hands, since they were in charge of my grades and could recommend me for honors classes, the key to a better life. It was all so simple then. And as young as I was, I understood how it worked. I believed my third-grade teacher Mrs. Flannagan when she told me that "readers are leaders" and that this would be the way out of my circumstances. I took that seriously and aimed to do everything possible to get out. That meant being "good" in school, getting good grades, and making the honor roll, never getting in trouble for being disruptive or disrespectful. I knew that these teachers were aware that I was a product of a single-parent home, so I wanted to make sure they knew that I was not like the rest of the people in this situation. I had this stuff in my head and no one could convince me otherwise. Aside from constant talking in class, I did well. Mrs. Flannagan's pale white Irish face would turn beet red when she told my mom that I was wonderful outside of the fact that I "talked and talked and talked and talked" (she tried to get every "talked" out in one breath).

Mrs. Flannagan never had to complain again because my mom dealt with me at home. Margarita was pretty intentional with her black belt. I hated that fucking belt. She never even wore it. That's why it was so offensive. She only kept it around to instill fear—and to beat my ass. It was a man's belt, it made discipline masculine to me. And I definitely also associated discipline with a dad. I would hear my friend Diana's mom say:

"When your father gets home, you're gonna get it!"

I knew that "it" was an ass whoopin'. And thanks to that belt, I got plenty of those. That was my dad at the time.

Because of my family dynamic, my view on family was specific. My family was made up of my grandmother, mother, and uncles, and that was it. I became very comfortable in that unit; it was all I knew. My mom was eighteen when we returned to the States to live with my grandmother in Miami. And though my mom was my mother, my grandmother was everyone's mother. I was so confused that I called my grandmother "Mami" and I called my mother by her first name. She was "Margarita" to me until I was about nine—by then, she beat it out of me.

My uncles were everything to me, they were always there for me. They walked me to school, took me out to eat, and every Sunday one of them would go to Comstock Park for a day jam and I would tag along. Uncle Carlos, the eldest, was three years older than my mother. He was our protector, the fighter. He was well respected in our neighborhood to the point where people were downright scared of him. My uncle Raymond, who was three years younger than my mom, was also very close to my mother. He knew that my father wasn't going to be around, so he got ahead of it and got a job to help. I don't think he liked school that much, so this was the perfect out. It was also what my uncles did to help the family.

Their relationships with my mom were both close but different. Carlos defended her in the streets and was always around to guide her. She learned how to fight from him; he made her tough. Raymond nurtured her in a very different way, he was her safe place. She could share her feelings and vulnerability with him and he was tender enough to receive it. He gave her the love and affection that she didn't feel from my grandmother.

Uncle Raymond was a closeted queer man, he had to uphold the machismo in our family and secretly pursue his deepest desires elsewhere. In our neighborhood the toxic messaging about homosexuality was deadly. He was the most paternal with me, he took care of me like I was his own and took the responsibility of parenting me very seriously. He told everyone that I was his daughter. He took me to school and made sure that I ate. I hated eating when I was a kid; it was a real problem. Aside from being anemic, I was also super skinny, and a thin kid was a sign of bad parenting in my community, so every family member took it upon themselves to make sure that I ate. Raymond would sit with me every day and spoon-feed me my dinner to make sure I finished it all.

There was also Uncle Richard, four years younger than my mom, the one I remember the least during my childhood. He was the first one to get out. He left home at sixteen, joined the Army, and never came back. As a ranked officer in the military with a master's degree, he became the success story of our family and had unknowingly set the road map for me. I would daydream about leaving, and he inspired me to believe that I was going to be a big star one day.

Uncle Pedro was five years younger than my mom. He was the lover, the one who always had girls chasing after him. When he was a teen, he was a sweet-talking, affectionate sap, who was also very expressive and kind with his words. I went to him when I wanted to hear how beautiful I was. And he was a great-looking human, usually described as a "typical Puerto Rican trigueño" with his dark brown skin, thick hair, and indigenous features. But it was his smile and how he called women "baby" that made him a hit. He was suave, it was effortless, girls were always fawning over him. When his high school sweetheart became the center of his life, he left the house, and then I would only see him on weekends.

My uncle Davie, six years younger than my mom, was the youngest and everyone treated him as the baby of the family. My grandmother coddled him likely without realizing she was actually stifling him, interrupting his growth and development. But he blossomed anyway, he was undeniable in his learning. He is probably one of the smartest people I have ever met, a self-taught electrician. I spent the most time with him because he was still at home. He introduced me to hip-hop, Muhammad Ali, Bruce Lee, and most important, Richard Pryor.

Richard Pryor was my first memory of laughing out loud at a comedian. I sat on the floor, hid behind the door, and listened to him tell his story about rescuing a dog that allowed burglars into his house and I cackled. Uncle Davie exposed me to the arts, he sparked my interest in performing. He is one of my favorite people on the planet and will still dance with me anytime, anywhere.

These were five men that I admired who also shared my last name. And although I was ashamed of not having my father's last name, they gave me pride in being a Rodriguez. I watched and learned so much from them—my biggest lessons were always in empathy. I saw them feed people who were on the street, defend ladies from getting mugged, and take care of my great-grandfather. A lot of people in my neighborhood were bullies, yet many times my uncles were there to the rescue. They never looked down on others or made fun of the vulnerable. They were and will always be my heroes, the Rodriguez brothers.

The older I got, the more I saw the flaws in my family. My uncles became human to me as I was more involved in their lives outside of home. My uncle Pedro had two sons with the girl he fell in love with. They were both barely in high school when they had their firstborn. Uncle Pedro had started to use drugs and things began to get bad for them. When she had her second son, my uncle was still getting high and becoming violent. Watching him hit her was the first time I could remember freezing in fear. Though I loved my uncle dearly, I believed that this was just what men did, but I also knew that what he was doing was wrong. Hearing that she deserved it from the women in my family was upsetting. Justifying him hitting her because she had a "smart mouth" was terrifying for me because I had been accused of having one too. It was conflicting because I loved them both. She was one of the most loving people in my life. Relief washed over me when they finally broke up because I wanted her to be safe and for my cousins to have a good life—they were like brothers to me. I also wanted my uncle to get clean.

My uncle Carlos had two children. He married the mother of his first child. I was jealous of that cousin of mine because she had married parents and her father's last name. I didn't know enough as a kid to acknowledge that she had a painful journey of her own. Her parents divorced when she was practically a baby. Her father spent more time around me than her and she didn't grow up with her little brother. My uncle passed away on his thirty-second birthday. His kids never really got to know him. I was left to fill in the blanks for them. I knew that they would have preferred to have him above anything else. I personally understood how they felt. But I have always tried my best to assure them of the big love he had for them. I believe that like most people in my family, he struggled with worthiness and self-esteem issues and felt that they were better off without him. It's likely the abuse he suffered as a kid was the reason he started to do drugs in the first place. I was too young to articulate to him that his kids needed him. I knew that firsthand. Regardless of what kind of person my father was, I needed him. Even if as adults we are able to understand that we are better off without some people in our lives, no one could convince us of that as kids.

My life shattered when Uncle Carlos died. He was the first person in my immediate family to go. I knew nothing of death at the time. How were we supposed to go on without him? I hurt so bad I became angry. He was a part of my whole, and it didn't work without him. Who was going to protect me now? I stood over his casket and opened his eyes. I didn't know anything about what they do with bodies after death, and no one had ever had any conversation with me about what happens to a person when they die, so when his eyes remained open, I insisted that he was still alive. I cried, kicked, and screamed, demanding that they wake him. My grandmother and mother were sedated, they couldn't deal with me. I just leaned on my uncles; as always, they took care of me. Watching them bury Uncle Carlos plays over in my head to this day. His absence created the very first hole in my heart, a blow that I will never forget. When I am in Miami, I go visit his grave and take him flowers, and will continue to do so until I go. I have never stopped missing him.

My uncle Richard took a different route. He was the one my grandmother said did things right. He met a girl while serving and fell in love. They got married and had a son. It was never anything to think about until they came to visit. Uncle Richard not only signed his son's birth certificate, but he stuck around. His family was the closest thing to what I saw on television. They were a military family who moved around, but they had a home. My cousin lived a good life, he had his own room and a pet dog. His life seemed peaceful and fun. They went on vacation and came to visit us on the way to or from Disney World. I had never been to Disney World as a little kid and we never went on trips nor visited any relatives. I didn't get to see them very much, so it was always a treat when they came over. They would take me with them to do things and eat at restaurants. Though at times I was jealous of their healthy family dynamic, I was very close to my cousin. I adoringly called him "my chicken," and he became my closest cousin. My feeling like a throwaway had nothing to do with him and I knew that. I just saw them and couldn't help but notice how broken my own family was. I romanticized my relationship with my uncle because he was part of my five-uncle unit, and idolized him because "he did things right," but in reality, I had not grown up around him and we didn't talk much. I was very close with my aunt. She stayed in touch and never forgot a special occasion—she has always been very thoughtful. At the end of the day, they were an example of what I wanted in my future.

In the sixth grade, I began to develop inside and out. I started to get attention from my teachers for being a leader and thriving academically. I was a tall girl and stood out and people started to notice me, even boys. I began to blossom in other ways and pursue the arts at school, auditioning for school plays and musicals. I actually booked a part in a school show that featured the music from the musical *Fame*. My mom could not believe it because I was so shy. I also ran for Student Council President and won. This was a new me and I liked it. I was more confident and had some excellent teachers. I had real support in school. I met my favorite teacher, Sylvia Rolle, the most beautiful woman I had ever seen. She had perfect white teeth and the most amazing dark brown skin. She was so perfect she looked unreal. She along with my sixth-grade teacher, Ms. Carter, really pushed me with my writing and performing. Ms. Rolle was my language arts teacher and was instrumental in my writing. Ms. Carter would always sing in class, she loved music. She encouraged me to use my voice to sing. It was the beginning of the performer in me. Even if I froze on stage, I kept going back for more. Something in me kept poking at me, there was something that I needed to discover in performance.

I also started to speak out, to use my words. I advocated for myself at school. I delivered my campaign speech with the same confidence that Bob Barker had hosting *The Price Is Right*. I was fascinated by anyone who used a microphone. I got tired of being bullied and began to stand up for myself. I had new friends and I was the funny one in the group. Angel, Maria, and Bambi were a big reason I wanted to go to school every day. I was feeling better about myself and I was having fun. I discovered that I had a voice and people were listening. Yet, in all of this newfound bliss, the one thing that bothered me, the one thing that still made me feel less than, was my struggle with illegitimacy.

Every single one of my friends had their father's last name and no matter how much I shined, I always felt that I was not enough.

I had a full-on fixation about not having my father's last name. My father's absence had now become the cause for anything that went wrong. It was easier to blame him, he was not around. I was never going to forgive him; I was mad. After all the torment I had felt for so long about being illegitimate, I finally gathered the courage to ask my mother why I didn't have his last name. As brave enough as I was to ask, I was definitely not ready for the answer. All the years of doubting his love for me, hating him for not validating me, recounting all of my worthiness issues, and everything I believed was connected to him not being there had boiled down to this very moment. I wanted to know.

"Why am I a 'Rodriguez'? Why didn't my father sign my birth certificate?"

And Margarita, being consistently who she is, looked at me with her signature ease and responded with her usual reckless abandon.

"He didn't want me to lose the welfare check."

It didn't even seem wrong to her; it was just how it was. Single moms and welfare checks were what she knew at the time. My grandmother had her six kids who were all Rodriguezes, and she received government assistance as well. Rather than ruin his situation, this grown man who couldn't get a job in the system because he didn't have legal status in the United States and was pursuing a dream of becoming a famous singer decided that the best way to help support us was by not ruining her chances for receiving any government aid. Seems like an abundance of bad choices being made and no one with enough sense to redirect us all. My grandmother was surviving and providing, my mother had no clue how she was going to live a life without someone else pulling the strings, and my father just didn't have his shit together. My uncles and I were the kids, we really couldn't do anything. I honestly began to believe that the stuff that happened to me was some sort of punishment from God because God didn't like me. I got used to it and it just became a part of who I was.

Pedro

One of the earliest memories I have of 3130, the building where I grew up, is a standoff between two women who were fighting for my uncle Pedro. He was a good-looking man with a Taino native look, about six foot two, very lean, brown skin, and dark hair. On top of being an attractive man, he was also very sweet and unafraid to share his feelings, as well as incredibly affectionate, especially with me. He would walk around with me on his shoulders or pick me up and spin me around, and he gave the best hugs. I find it important to point this out there because there's so much machismo in my culture, in my family, that men are celebrated for being dry and stoic. My uncle Pedro defied all of that while maintaining his masculinity, which was celebrated because he had women—girlfriends of all sizes, races, and personalities.

I had always been aware of my uncle and his relationships. I was always around them, nothing was ever kept from me. He had been in a relationship with Chita for eight years. Chita was a Puerto Rican girl from another neighborhood whom he met at school and immediately fell in love. She was tiny, sweet, but very aggressive and feisty, and had the longest hair I had ever seen—it hit below her knees. Her tresses matched the beautiful brown eyes on her thin face—the IG face before the internet. She and Uncle Pedro were in a relationship well into high school, where they had their first child. He was born right after my brother, so we had two babies in the family now.

As time passed, Pedro and Chita began to develop a volatile relationship. They would argue and fight anywhere. He would joke and say that it was her hormones. She was around my mom's age, maybe a little bit younger, and she was always ready for the fight. She had her own issues from home and refused to be called by her real name, Consuelo. In her mind, she left it behind with the bad things that happened to her there. She never spoke of those things, but we knew what they were—most of us had experienced similar situations. It usually felt like . . . "Whatever happened when I couldn't help it, did, but fuck with me now and see what happens." Her trauma put her perpetually on the defensive.

Even so, I loved her so much and she loved me back. She was someone who defended me and treated me like she had been there my entire life. My mom trusted her with me because she knew that she would protect me at all costs. One day when she and a friend picked me up from the bus stop, they saw when an older girl bumped into me on purpose as I was getting off the bus. The girl thought it was amusing to mow me over and then laugh it off with her friends. My new aunt Chita immediately jumped on the girl and when they tumbled off the bus, Chita's friend jumped in to help fight her and her three-girl crew until they couldn't take it anymore. I just stood there and watched the scuffle, hoping to get home soon so I could do my homework. Seeing people fight had become normal to me.

Chita had her first son at sixteen and a year later had baby number two. She and Uncle Pedro were barely eighteen when their relationship began to fall apart, and now there were these two children in the mix. They were constantly quarreling and my uncle was using drugs. It made him someone else, someone abusive and angry. Nothing like the uncle I was used to. Had I not seen it for myself, I would not have believed it. They loved each other very much, so much that they made two beautiful children. But they were also very young and immature and misguided and needed help. Eventually, the police came to their house one too many times and she left him.

Pedro never recovered from the breakup. He still loved Chita, but she moved on. He continued to do drugs and now he had more reason to numb himself, just like my uncle Carlos. Pedro became a revolving door of women in our old inner-city Miami apartment building. And since a lot of my family members occupied apartments at the same time, they did not go unnoticed. At the time, I lived in apartment 6, which was located on the second floor of that two-story building. My great-grandfather lived in apartment 9 and my uncles Pedro and Carlos lived in apartment 4. There was a set of stairs on each side of the building and the hallways had concrete floors that had to be mopped to keep clean. One day, as I was playing jacks on the floor outside my apartment, I heard someone call out, "Aidita!" Aidita was my family nickname and only those who were closest to my family knew to call me that. When I looked up, it was Rosa, a hot Puerto Rican girl from the neighborhood. She and I were not that close, so she was definitely taking liberties with my name. She stood at about five foot one and weighed no more than eighty-something pounds. She had long jet-black hair, and mild acne, and always wore a huge smile. When I say huge smile, I mean she had really big teeth. She was the sister of LJ and Brian, who were the drug-dealing loan sharks in our neighborhood who would go around trying to break people's legs when they didn't get paid. I hated them. I believe that at some point, when it was my uncle Pedro's turn to get beat up for not paying his loan back, they bartered their sister. She had been in love with my uncle forever and they wanted someone to marry her and take her off their hands. That's what my mom said. Pedro didn't really like her like that, she was just someone to hang out with at the time. But she fell hard for him and she started to come around more and more. She was trying to build a relationship while he was working off a debt.

"Is your uncle home?" asked Rosa that day.

"No," I replied without hesitation. My answer was always no. I knew the rules. We were to never divulge any information about the family. Plus, I had just gotten home from school and was getting ready for our afternoon kickball game, I didn't have time to get in trouble.

Unfortunately, there was another woman at my uncle's door that day: Jessie, a white girl from Homestead, which was right outside of Miami. She was five foot ten, thicker-bodied, and had a beautiful face with blue eyes, blond hair, and a crooked smile. She was very nice to me but I didn't know her very well. In many ways, she was a stranger. Up to this point, the only white people I had encountered were on television and a few teachers in my school. They were from a different world.

These two women arrived at the same time and were now banging on my uncle's apartment door. We all knew he was in there, and we knew that he knew they were out there and was purposefully not opening the door, so they tried to get me to talk. But I knew better than to give out any information. The other thing we all knew was Jessie had an invitation and Rosa, a glutton for pain, just showed up. She knew he was seeing other people. Shit, I knew, and I was eight.

I had seen this type of standoff between two women in front of Uncle Pedro's apartment—it was nothing out of the ordinary in my neighborhood. Jessie was all up in Rosa's face going off on her, and Rosa just stood there and cried, that was definitely a no-no. She lost major street cred with those tears and would definitely have to answer to the block later. Jessie didn't come from the street; she came from a two-parent home in a middle-class suburban neighborhood, but she had some issues with substance abuse, and she was fearless. She also liked the bad boys, which was why she was in the inner city of Miami banging on a man's door fighting off a Puerto Rican girl who grew up there.

She won the fight and the guy that day. After hours of bickering, my uncle finally came out and sent Rosa home. Pedro and Jessie became an official couple.

We went to her house for dinner once, a meal we would never forget. They invited my grandmother and her husband over for dinner and I tagged along. Jessie was cooking stroganoff, a departure from the rice and beans I ate every day, so I was excited to try it. American food, as my family called it, was something that I craved because I ate Latin food daily. As we settled into the evening and got comfortable, my grandmother went into the kitchen to grab a drink, and we heard a loud scream. I jumped up from my seat and ran over to her, thinking something awful had happened. When I got to my grandmother, her arm was stretched out in front of her with a glass in her hand and she was frozen in place as if someone had forgotten to say, "green light." Turns out, she'd casually pulled it out of the cupboard and when she went to pour some lemonade into the glass, she noticed something at the bottom: cat shit. Their cats would wander about the kitchen and whoever was on kitchen duty that day had missed a glass. I found the whole scene hilarious, but my grandmother immediately took it as confirmation that these two just didn't fit. It wasn't that they were racially, culturally, or ethnically different, there was just something about their personalities that didn't seem to mesh. The relationship felt forced and there was always some sort of confusion, conflict, or weirdness whenever we were around them, like that night with the cat shit in the glass. My grandmother refused to eat the stroganoff after this incident and I knew the relationship was now doomed. Aida was the matriarch, most of us followed her lead, especially Uncle Pedro. She was the apple of his eye, the one woman he loved unconditionally throughout his life. Jessie lost my grandmother that day and, soon after that, my uncle Pedro. Her to the cat and him to the drugs.

For someone who was just in the third grade, it seemed like a lot for me to take in, but it was also something that I had seen before. The roles of women were defined by the men in my circle. My uncles revered my grandmother and protected and respected my mom. I was treasured and adored. Every other woman had to earn her respect and fighting for a man was never it. Even I knew it was lame and I was a little girl.

My uncle Pedro would later get clean and sober and become a counselor for those who struggle with addiction. He is still the sweetest man and now an amazing father and husband. Witnessing his evolution has been wonderful. He is definitely one of the success stories in my family that I am most proud of.

Pizza and Penis

I remember feeling alone in my childhood. My uncles were around, but they were getting older. I was four, playing jacks and hopscotch, and my youngest uncle, Davie, was listening to hip-hop and kissing girls. We were definitely not in the same place, and even though he always entertained me, it always felt like my uncle had a role of authority in my life. He was not my friend or playmate, more like a young adult who took time to look after his little niece.

"I got kidnapped twice. I was hot in these streets . . . my mother stole me from my father, it was a basic parental kidnap. And my grandmother stole me from my mother because she was dating a killer."

This evolved into the joke that summed up my first five years on the planet, and is one of the most relatable jokes of my Netflix special. It is funny, but what doesn't come across in the joke is how traumatic the experience was for me.

My mom started dating again. She was still so young, barely

twenty, and all she wanted was true love. Who was I to stand in the way? The hopeless romantic who raised me made sure that I, too, went looking for the fairy tale later in my own life, but we'll get there soon enough. After the bad stuff my mom had gone through with my father, she was now in search of someone who really got her, loved her, and had her back. I couldn't wait to have a dad—I remember hoping that one would show up. I wanted a man for my mom too. She needed someone to take some of the weight off her shoulders, to help with responsibilities. We both needed that person.

Out one night with her brothers, she met a guy. He was big, strong, dark, and Asian—a Puerto Rican who had roots somewhere outside of the Caribbean. Many of us do . . . the gifts of colonization that keep on giving. They called him "El Coreano" (The Korean). Usually, anyone who is Asian is rounded off as being Chinese among Latinos, and occasionally Korean. He was quiet and mysterious; there was definitely a story.

The relationship came at us fast and hard. They immediately became a couple and were inseparable from that point forward. My mother was in love, she was completely taken by this guy. He was funny, loving, and protective, and that was all she thought she needed. She bragged about how he was willing to punch anyone in the face for her. I don't think any man had made her feel so safe up to this point in her life other than my uncle Carlos. My father definitely hadn't, and she made mention of this constantly. I felt safe around El Coreano too. He looked like he could beat anyone up. I didn't know any better.

They'd barely been together for a year when my mom got pregnant. I was confused because they weren't married. Where did this baby come from? I didn't know exactly how a child was conceived, but I knew you needed a woman and man to do it. Nonetheless, I was ecstatic because I was going to get what I had been waiting for: a brother. There was no ultrasound or confirmation from the doctor. I just knew it was a boy. I started calling her stomach my brother as soon as her bump became visible. I didn't really care about how it came to be. Now that my uncles were getting older and starting their own families, I didn't have anyone to do life with and I spent a lot of time alone. My brother was going to be my best friend.

El Coreano was around all the time. When my mother fell, she fell hard, she wanted to have her own family so bad. He soon moved into our apartment and I got wrapped up in the fantasy of what a family was with her. The life that I was used to with my grandmother and uncles was interrupted, things were changing faster than I could digest them. But where my mother went, I followed. This was different, though. The only men I was used to being around were my uncles and now El Coreano began to call me his daughter. He said he didn't want me to feel different from the baby on the way. We were equal in his eyes, both his. I felt loved in an odd sense. I barely knew this man but I was finally going to have a dad. My family was now my mommy, my brother, and my bonus father. My mother's pregnancy came with a lot for her and too much for me. We suddenly moved to New York with El Coreano and left everyone I knew and loved back in Miami.

Everything I knew about New York I learned through TV, movies, and songs. I knew it to be a cool place that was fast-paced and filled with people like me, Puerto Ricans and Latinos who looked like me, so I did my best to look forward to my new life. After all, this was the place where all the stars were, the ones I knew who came from our island, the Fania All Stars and Coco from *Fame*. As we settled in, my mom tried to make the best of things, but our situation was anything but ideal. In fact, it was nowhere near normal. I was hopping around with my pregnant mother, staying at a cheap Bronx motel, where the super would try to sneak a peek at my mom through a fire escape window. Why wasn't my new father living with us and providing us with protection twenty-four hours a day? We had a weirdo peeping through our window. We spent most of our time by ourselves in this cold place. At home in Miami, anytime I went outside to play with the other kids, I was supervised by either my grandmother or one of my uncles. But in New York there was no one watching us. We were out in the world and this man who was supposed to be our family was never around.

He lived somewhere else because he was on the run for murder. I learned that shortly after our move to the city. No matter how much my mom tried to keep things from me, I always found them out somehow. There wasn't much of a filter among her new circle of friends. They actually took it upon themselves to look out for us: a pregnant woman with a little girl. We were vulnerable and there wasn't anyone visibly around to defend us, so they helped as much as they could. Willie was an addict who lived on the streets and loved my mom, so he'd always make sure that we got to the motel safely.

On one of those cold winter nights, this opportunistic pig of a super, who took advantage of knowing we were alone, was trying to check my mom out while she changed and Willie saw and reported back to El Coreano. The next night he poked his head through the window while standing on the fire escape and El Coreano caught the creep in action. The fire escape was how my new stepfather would come up to visit us, to avoid coming into contact with people in the building. He was on the news and he was wanted, he couldn't afford to use the front door. That night, the super almost became victim number two; he beat that man up so hard his body dangled over the rail as he begged for mercy. And I saw the whole thing. That is why he didn't kill him, because I was watching. I saved his life. I remember not feeling bad for him, he violated us, he deserved it. I had seen so many vigilante movies at this point, I thought that was how it worked.

Because of this incident, we had to go. That man called the police and we left. We relocated to a cold-ass basement that was located in the house of a strange Dominican woman. She was the sister of a good friend of my grandmother's. Miss Celia was tall and brown and had an accent that was different from the people in my family—she was Dominican—but she felt familiar to me. She rocked a full set of rollers and always wore tight Gloria Vanderbilt jeans. I remember them because I wanted a pair. The day I met her she had on a flamingo-pink tight shirt tucked in the jeans to match. She was happy to see me and was so affectionate from the very beginning, giving hugs and kisses like she had known me my whole life. It was strange, not only because I didn't really know her but also because I was not used to that level of affection. She was a pretty lady with an unnerving laugh that sounded like a bird noise I heard once while watching *Animal Kingdom*.

Miss Celia invited us into her home without any hesitation, she insisted on it. Meanwhile, although my mom was suspicious of the connection with my grandmother's friend and this lady, she was in a bad situation and she owned it. It was the first time my mother really felt like she was on her own, because she was. Even though she was in a relationship, El Coreano was never really around. Up against the wall, she felt the best choice was to accept this lady's offer and move into her house.

The place was cool, way better than that crappy motel room we had been living in. Her house smelled like food and I liked that. I still wasn't eating all that much, but I enjoyed a home-cooked meal, it felt like love. There was a record player, a TV, and pictures of her family in the Dominican Republic. Her couch was loud, it was a burgundy color with the plastic on it. She had two bird figurines that I couldn't stop staring at—I was so curious about why people had fake animals in their homes. Why not just get the real thing? Her home felt safe above all things and I knew when I got there that I wanted to stay. I was tired of running around. I loved my mother and although I didn't want to keep doing this, I just really couldn't bear the thought of not being with her either. So it was important to me that she wanted to be there too.

There was something very calming about Celia, she would rub my back and make me feel like everything was okay. I really needed that at the time. I was a bag of bones, pretty shifty, or as my family would refer to me, "a nervous kid." Having the assurance from someone stable enough to lend us the roof over her head gave her the credibility of someone that I could depend on. It didn't take much at the time. She had a deep concern for my mother, and she wore that on her face. When my mom would go out, she would ask her what time she was coming back and to let her know where she was going. She would even ask if she wanted her to babysit me. My mom would always say no. I think that she already felt like a burden and didn't want to add to the load. Besides, she didn't want it to get back to my grandmother that she was leaving me behind. There was so much judgment around motherhood in my family. My grandmother and mother had the rule book on what a "good" mother was. There was always an evaluation taking place on how someone was taking care of their kids. It didn't take much, all you had to do was make sure they ate, had clothes and a roof over their head, and that they weren't molested. I was grateful to my mother for keeping me alive, since I believed that this was the main task required of parenthood. Miss Celia knew that my mom's man was on the run. It was a supposed secret, but everyone knew. It was obvious and also common. Celia was concerned about us too. My mom acted like she was in a romance novel, not in a horror film. They were a modern-day Bonnie and Clyde with a kid in tow. I remember them kissing in public and holding hands. Nevertheless, she convinced me that we were a family, even if we were on the run.

But things were still bad. My mother's pride wouldn't allow her to let Celia take care of us, so we had to go out and beg for food in the street. One cold night when I was hungry and tired, we went to a nightclub in Washington Heights and sat outside on the sidewalk. We ended up there because Miss Celia had run into El Coreano there and caught him partying with other women, so my mother wanted to catch him in the act. He never came out so she started to ask everyone who came out for money to get us food. This beautiful Black man saw us and came back with two slices of pizza. His accent was familiar, he sounded like my family back home in Miami. The highlight of being a panhandler was getting a slice of pizza but for my mom it was more than that. The pizza was a gift from the famous Puerto Rican singer Ismael Miranda. I had no idea who that man was at the time, I was just thankful to be eating. I was getting tired of our situation and wanted us to go back home to family-cooked meals and the heat. Instead I sat on the cold ground with a slice being the only thing I had to look forward to, knowing that once it was gone, the next meal would become another adventure. I was four and tall for my age, yet I barely weighed fifty pounds and had bags under my eyes. I wasn't much of an eater but this hunger made me miss my grandmother's food, especially the oatmeal she made for breakfast, it was my favorite. Her oatmeal was special. She ground the dry oats in her blender before cooking it. The result was a magic, creamy, buttery, sweet, delicious goodness. I remember especially missing the feeling of warmth when I ate it. I yearned for my grandmother that night. After the pizza, we returned to Celia's to sleep. My mom never wanted to impose so we would usually leave the house early in the morning and come back right at bedtime. I was constantly exhausted and moments like getting that slice were usually the best thing in my days.

That night, El Coreano was waiting for us at the door. He'd do this, he'd come by from time to time to hang out with us as if he was doing us a favor and it was a treat. He loved to rub my mother's belly and talk to the baby. I was over it and checked out. This was definitely not how my ideal family played out in my head. He did spend time with me during those impromptu visits. We'd play hot hands and patty-cake while my mom took a shower. Oftentimes, he'd bring junk food—chips, Now and Laters, or soda—but not this particular night. We stayed downstairs in the basement, being quiet as instructed, we didn't want to get kicked out of there. I know I didn't; this basement was my safe haven in New York.

I was a pretty calm kid, I played with my toys and read books. I was an only kid up to this point, and I was used to being alone. I would read the Bible, which was not by choice. My mom was very much into Christianity, she was a believer. And like many Christians she would justify just about anything with scripture. Like a man killing another man in self-defense, that was an "eye for an eye." Even though the story went that a man pulled a gun on him and he took the gun away and shot him anyway. That was not self-defense, that was murder. Pure ego.

We'd go down to the Pentecostal church to sing hymns and get food and beg for forgiveness. My mom would pray long and hard and cry. Asking for a way out and I followed her lead. I was hoping that Jesus would show up. Life was trash at this point. Being in that basement was a constant reminder of this. Even though it was the place I preferred to be in while in New York, I knew it was still bad. I had to keep myself entertained and occupied because I was pretty down. I remember feeling depressed, even at this age. Looking back and being able to acknowledge that is important because I have always identified it as an adult thing, and there I was feeling it at a very young age, most of the time.

This night, the one my mom met one of her favorite singers, turning it into one of the best moments in my mom's life to date, was also one of the times I can still vividly remember her being happy in New York. As she went off to the bathroom humming one of his songs, I decided to play jacks, one of my favorite games because I usually played it with my mom, and it would bring out the little girl in her. So I played alone, waiting for her to return. I couldn't go to sleep without her. As I threw down the pieces and bounced the ball to pick them up, I heard my name being whispered. My new father was calling me. I didn't think anything of it, since we were supposed to be quiet when we were in Celia's house, so I turned around to respond and couldn't quite get what was happening. When I focused in his direction, I saw him holding a part of his body in his hand that I had never seen before. It had an odd shape and seemed spiny. Whatever it was, I wanted no part of it. This was the first time I was introduced to anything sexual. My uncles were constantly around and I don't remember them so much as being wrapped in a towel after a shower. I know that they felt helpless because they weren't able to protect my mom from her abuser, so they were diligent with me. I was their second chance and they never let their guard down. But they weren't there while this was happening, I had to figure this one out on my own.

Time stopped, and I had to make a decision, one more thing for me to have to survive as a kid. "¿Quieres tocarlo?" he said, asking me if I wanted to touch it. I froze. In fact, I freeze thinking about it now. It was as if my entire body was stuck. That emotional paralysis would soon become a constant in my life. The man who made me feel like his daughter and was protective and nurturing was just grooming me, waiting for the right moment to make his move. As he made his way toward me I became unstuck. I had a sense that a terrible thing was coming for me. My mom was so into him I wasn't really sure how she would react—she was blinded by him and let him get away with so much. He was probably grooming her too. My heart jumped out of my chest and I ran for it. Once I reached the first step of the staircase, I knew I was out of there. I hopped up one by one and, when I reached the top, I sprinted into Celia's room. I stood inside her door and just stared at her. That lady knew what was going on without me having to say one word. She patted her bed gesturing for me to climb in and I jumped right in. She then cradled me while I cried myself to sleep. When my mom came to get me, Celia covered for me. She said she'd gone to get me to watch a kid show on TV and then I'd fallen asleep. She reassured my mom I could stay until the morning. I think my mom knew something weird had happened but she wasn't able to deal with it. She was pregnant and swollen everywhere, and there was so much else going on. But she knew I was safe with this lady; she was in my grandmother's tribe and they looked out for each other. Celia told her to take advantage of the privacy that night and go enjoy some time with her man. She didn't send me back to my mom until the next morning when she was sure he was gone. She gave me a hug and told me I could sleep in her bed anytime.

The next day, church became more than a snack center. I needed to repent; I felt like I had done something wrong, as if it was my fault this man tried to get me to touch his stuff. So I stayed on my knees extra-long asking God to forgive me that day. My mom was proud and happy to see me really getting into it. She saw my behavior as a sign of growth. It was as if she had completely forgotten the night before and I was still right in the middle of it. I was in the pew feeling sick to my stomach, I couldn't explain that then. I just *knew*. The women in my life taught me that we were innately evil, the Bible said so. They hated themselves and other women and now I was joining in. Every time they spoke of adultery, rape, and any other wrongdoing, it was always the woman's fault. Why would this be any different? All the bad stuff happening in my life suddenly registered as my punishment for what had happened the night before. It didn't make sense, but I was a little girl and I was lost and I needed Jesus to save me. From this point forward I dedicated my life to the Lord, I became my mother's very own pastor. She would lie in the bed elevating her swollen ankles while I recited passages from the Bible and sang my favorite hymns. She was filled with joy while I was basking in shame.

A few nights after the incident, Celia asked to babysit so my mother could go on a date with her man. She had become more involved and was helping out, especially with me. My mother didn't want to leave me that night but El Coreano convinced her to. He stopped speaking to me and was very brief and dry; it was as if he didn't even know me.

After they were gone, Celia began scrambling around her apartment like a mad woman. It was as if she was in a hurry. She rushed me down to the basement and dressed me in several layers—it was really cold that night. We then went back upstairs, she put one of her scarves around my neck, and we sat in her living room to watch TV, as if I wasn't dressed for the North Pole. I was a little kid, so it didn't take much to distract me. I started to watch *El Chavo del Ocho*, a comedy sketch show that I would watch with my grandma. I chuckled and it was as if I heard my abuela laughing with me. I missed her so much that I started to hear her voice from time to time. That night I looked around because I felt her presence and even thought I saw her. I smelled the Red Door perfume she always wore. My mind was really playing tricks on me, there was no way. Abuela was in Miami and I was here in hell. Then I heard her voice again and this time I stood up. I had to investigate. I looked over at Celia who was smiling from ear to ear as she gestured over to her right. This was not a mirage of my favorite Aida. It was actually her! She had come to rescue me, I just knew it. I ran as fast as I could, grabbed her, and never wanted to let her go. I cried and buried my head into her shoulder, taking in the scent that I used to complain about. Now it was the fragrance of liberation. I would finally be free from the horror that was that man—my grandmother was here to take me home.

Celia had only been letting us stay with her out of allegiance to my grandmother. She hadn't disclosed to my grandmother that we were there because she was giving my mom some time to work things out. But a line had been crossed when El Coreano violated me and she was not going to allow it to go any further. She made the call and my grandmother immediately jumped into action. After that night, my mom always said my grandmother loved me more than her because she came to get me. I believed differently, this was also an act of love for her daughter, an apology and atonement. She didn't know how to say she was sorry, she couldn't own up to her own shortcomings, so she did this instead.

My grandmother carefully plotted with my uncle Raymond when she got the phone call from Celia. They knew that they had to get me out of there; it was only bound to get worse. Celia was all in. She served my grandma a cup of coffee to go as she handed me over. Those two had a silent agreement, they had a code. All I remember was feeling safe with them both. They were strength and power. I gave Celia the tightest hug that night, as if I already knew I would never see her again, and a few hours later, my grandmother and I checked into a hotel in Chinatown. It would be the first night that I slept in total peace, not even thinking about my mom. I had no idea of the pain she would feel when she returned and I was not there. The next morning we went shopping. As I changed into new clothes, Abuela threw away what I took off. In one day we were all over the city. She took me to a Dominican hair salon in Washington Heights and had all my hair cut off. I remember asking, "Are we going to go get my mom?" And my grandmother quickly replied, "She'll come later." Next thing I knew I was wearing a green jumper with some Bruce Lee shoes—the little soft black shoes with a strap—and I looked like an entirely different kid. In no time, we were at the airport boarding a flight and heading down to Miami back to my real family. I was so sad to leave my mama, but I really couldn't take the struggle anymore. I had been cold, hungry, tired, and molested, it was time for me to go. She sobbed loudly when we talked on the phone the night I got back to my grandma's place. I felt guilty hearing her cry, but somehow I knew that it was best for me. I had to go to school and get back to being a kid. Running around with a convict who asked me to touch his penis was not part of the plan.

It was a tough year without my mother, a lot of crying and pleading with her to come back over the phone. I remember vividly the pain and loss I felt without her and the fear that something would happen to her. When my mom finally returned to Miami, she brought my brother with her. I had spent what felt like an eternity without her and I also felt bad that I wasn't around when my baby brother was born. I was supposed to be there for him and my mom. She needed me. But now we were together again, this was a good moment for us, I couldn't believe she was back. She was so happy to be with her two children, I could feel her relief. She was safe. I was so happy to see her too—that woman was my whole heart. Thanking Jesus left and right, I prayed that the Lord would permanently rid us of that man—he brought bad stuff to our lives. I wanted my little brother to be safe. The positive feelings for El Coreano quickly faded away. What he did to me was not what a father does to his daughter, I was sure of it. And I was now petrified that he would come back somehow and do something to my brother.

My mom's return was the best thing for me. I was having nightmares about my mother dying, a recurring dream of me at a cemetery crying over her grave. My grandmother would tell her on their calls while she was gone that she needed to come back because I was suffering. I heard her say that this man was going to lead my mom to a prison or an early grave. Hearing that fed the dreams even more. I cried for my mother a lot while I was awake. Her coming back made me feel so much better. I had her back and that was all that mattered. I now had my own brother, too. They were my family. He and I were going to re-create what my uncles had growing up. I had dreamed of the day and now it was finally here.

My mom eventually got a new place and we started over. She stopped talking about the man who tainted what was supposed to be one of the most joyous events of a woman's life. She told us that the way she went into labor was a nightmare. I was so glad that she was finally getting over him. Once we were settled in our new place and finally started to move forward, El Coreano came to visit one day, claiming that he wanted to see his kids. I froze as he stood in the doorway. Why was he back? Wasn't he in New York? I had been such a good girl. Did God not listen to my prayers? When he reached over to me for a hug, all I could do was flinch. It was as if nothing ever happened, he was back to being a dad and I was stuck yet again.

He would come by from time to time, you could smell the desperation on him. His time was running out and he was tired of fleeing. He was trying to work his way back into our lives. On this particular day, I was playing with my toy soldiers as my uncle Carlos read his newspaper on the couch. I sat at his feet, another safe place. When El Coreano walked in the door and grabbed me for a hug, chills crawled up my spine to the back of my neck. My uncle never knew what happened, we were told never to tell my uncles because they would "catch a case." As men of color, they'd never receive any grace from the justice system. I understand now, but back then I was just told not to say anything because if I did, my uncle would go to jail. And again, it would be my fault. So when the creep forced that hug on me, there was nothing I could do but hug back.

My mother was using the bathroom and he didn't wait, he just went into the bedroom to see my brother. He sat on the bed staring at the baby, while I kept my eye on him from the doorway. I didn't trust him. I knew he loved his son but he was still a wild card. My mom was taking longer than usual; I assume she was avoiding him. He kept making attempts at getting back with her, but she was tired of his shit. Like a scene from a movie, time stood still, and even though there was activity taking place, it felt silent. Until a loud thump at the door broke it all up—a sound I never heard before and will never forget. It was loud, it made my heart race, and before I could process what was happening, my uncle snatched me, the door was kicked open, and a bunch of men dressed like the toy soldiers that had fallen out of my hand rushed in. My uncle tossed me behind the couch while my mom ran out of the bathroom with her hands up and yelled, "I have my kids in the house!" El Coreano came out of the bedroom holding my baby brother, I just wailed. I really didn't know what he was going to do, but I knew what he was capable of. I felt so helpless. My uncle knew the drill, he was face down on the ground and my mom, hysterical, reached for her baby. Guns pointed at everyone, one officer gently grabbed the baby from his father's arms and handed him to my mom, and El Coreano went quietly. Before leaving the apartment, he looked back at us and told me that he loved me. He then turned to my mother and added, "Espera por mí," *wait for me*. The room went silent again and all I heard was the clasp of the handcuffs. As the last officer stepped out of our apartment, I finally let out a sigh of relief. It was over. My mom and I had peace. I don't know who made the call, but I was so grateful. I felt like Jesus and I had a direct connection at that moment, he had finally answered my prayer.

China and Black and the Green Machine

At five years old, I watched *Diff'rent Strokes* with my uncles and I loved it. It became my favorite show, it was funny and about family. Arnold and Willis made me want a little brother. I needed a best friend and someone to play and hang with and I wanted someone to take care of. I had been through some things in my life and I was going to make sure that my baby brother didn't. He was the first person that I actually wanted to protect.

I wasn't there when my brother was born, I was in Miami, he was born in New York. The pacing around the hospital floor, the doctor coming out telling the rest of the family, "It's a boy!"—those didn't happen for me. I didn't get the opportunity to jump up and down or throw my suggestions for a name in the hat. My grandmother had taken me to Miami and I left my first sibling with a surrogate family of prostitutes and junkies. My brother's arrival was not the best. He was born days after El Coreano beat our mother. He cheated on her, and when she found out and confronted him, he didn't appreciate her tone or questioning and decided to teach her a lesson. He beat a nine-months-pregnant woman and left her for dead in Central Park. And those people, who many saw as undesirables in society, were the ones to take care of her and deliver her to the nearest hospital, saving both her and her baby's lives. To this very day she says, "Never look down on anyone, it was the prostitutes and junkies that rescued us."

My little brother was born in the middle of the night. I remember the call. I had school the next day, but I couldn't go back to sleep. I felt guilty for not being there.

Having a young mother who had her own rule book for parenting came with lots of challenges. She learned from my grandmother to operate in survival mode, we felt that. It was an exhausting way to live, waiting for something bad to happen, always being on guard. Fighting so that people would respect you enough to leave you alone is heavy, especially when you're a kid. Believing that men are superior was especially hard to understand, after all, I was surrounded by strong women. Witnessing the men in our lives do horrible things to the women I adored, hitting them, scamming them, and cheating was awful. And in turn, the women protected those same men from the consequences. It was not fair. These were the values that I was being handed down from my role models.

I was still taking care of my mother in my mind because I was afraid to lose her again. That feeling has never gone away. At that young age, I took on my mother's load, from her sexual abuse as a child to her dysfunctional relationships with men, and I made excuses for her. She told me about her molestation when I was five as a cautionary tale, never taking into account what it was doing to me as a little girl who was dealing with trauma of her own. And she constantly reminded me that no one on the planet ever had it as bad as she did. It made me want to try to make it all better.

Taking care of her meant looking out for my brother, making sure that he was always safe. I made sure that he ate, didn't get hurt, and was protected from being molested. I met him when he was six months old and he was the most beautiful baby I had ever seen. I would beg to hold him, since I believed that I had the safest hands he could ever be in. I stalked him. I loved him as a baby, I would pretend that he was mine. I would jump in his crib and give him his bottle. I would stare at him and rub his head. He made my life hell at times. We lived in a one-bedroom apartment and a loud baby crying through the night meant I became the jumpy kid at school with bags under my eyes due to the lack of sleep—I have the school pictures to prove it. I would still rush home every day to see him, I would sit on a chair and hold him for as long as I could.

As he got older, my brother, like any other, became a pain in the ass. He wanted everything I had, broke all my shit, and cried when he didn't get his way. He was learning the power he wielded over our mom. My little brother had slanted eyes and looked more Asian than anything, so everyone called him Chino. My mother called him China, that was her nickname for him, she adored him. He was her favorite; they had a special bond. She had been through so much while she was pregnant with him. She had a tender place in her heart for him. I did too. As he got older and became a toddler, he got away with a lot. She felt guilty for what she put herself through during her pregnancy and compensated by overprotecting him. *Give it to him, he was born in New York alone, no one was around.* I expected more from her. Did she think my life had been a party? I often felt overlooked but I still adored my brother; it was her I started to resent. She was a victim herself, twenty-two with two kids from two fathers who were not around. She tried her best, that is all she could do. We all needed help and protection.

My baby brother and I formed an inexplicable bond. Despite our age difference, he became my best friend. We managed to have our own fun while surviving. Our mom was sad, our uncles were scattered doing different things in life and had started to go out and drink. It was just us a lot of the time. I would sit in the room and do my homework while my brother played with his toys. I loved him so much, I believed he came straight from heaven. I was still a kid but I quickly also felt like his second mom, or at least I'd play the part.

We grew together. I couldn't wait for the day when he got old enough to go outside to play with me, and when he did, he'd go under my supervision because he was only two and I was responsible for him. We ran around our buildings, free from home, skipping against the wind. We played kickball and tag and every outdoor game you could imagine. He was a fast learner; he didn't have a choice. The kids in our neighborhood ranged in ages, ethnicities, and economic backgrounds. There were mostly Caribbean kids, Puerto Ricans and Dominicans and Cubans, and a few from Honduras and Nicaragua. At eight, I was one of the older kids, the youngest being around three, until my brother came along at two. Our block was mixed with apartments for rent and houses owned by early settlers who came from everywhere. We were kids and we all played together, even if the adults didn't mix. All we cared about was who was going to be on our team.

China was very athletic and you could see it early on. He loved to run, and he was fast. As he got older, he got good at all the games. And with that came competitiveness and other things we learned that started to steal our innocence away. The parents weren't any better at teaching valuable lessons, they just added fuel to the fire. It was as if the kids' performance was an extension of them. They projected their rivalries on us when we just wanted to play. Our fun started to get ruined because they started to come watch our games. Cheering, heckling, and arguing is how they supported us. It was awful. After all, playing outside was our escape from them. Now they were right there egging us on. Javier and Manny were in constant competition with China, and their mother, Naomi, would instigate, "You're gonna let that little kid outrun you, Javi? You're faster than him!" It would not stop and the arguments among the parents were absolutely ridiculous. They bet on who was going to the major leagues as if they were on the draft committee. This started to cause dissent among us.

We weren't getting along like we used to and these games, which we were now being forced to play, had become just another chore.

One day after school as we were gearing up for a kickball game, I couldn't find China anywhere. I was terrified, I was going to get in so much trouble if something happened to him. My mom watched the news daily and always reported back to us all the bad things that were happening, like the rise in kidnappings across the country. "They are taking all the kids, not just the white ones," she'd tell us with despair. So, after calling for my brother to no avail, I dropped the ball and went looking for him. I ran around the building with sweaty palms and heavy breath, but he was nowhere to be seen. I knew our mom would start calling for us soon and I was not in the mood for a beating.

I walked to the back of our building, and heard a sound off to the corner of our parking lot. I saw kids huddled but couldn't spot my brother. I went in closer and realized that Manny and Javier and their older sister were hovering over China, beating him up. Their older sister, Dina, was covering his mouth while her brothers pummeled him. My baby bro cried and tried to fight back but he was outnumbered. I saw red, I was angry, my stomach dropped. I was filled with rage and charged them all. First, I grabbed Dina by her long hair and slung her to the floor. Then I took turns punching the boys in the head. There was no technique, just anger. They fought back, Javier punched me while Manny bit, and Dina pulled my hair, they all piled up on me. I eventually fought them all off and grabbed my brother by the hand. We ran toward the entrance of our building but before we could reach the stairs we slammed right into Naomi, the most divisive mom on the block, she always caused drama for the kids.

My mother started calling for us while I stood in front of Naomi, a big woman from Honduras with an open-face gold crown tooth who always wore green eye shadow and very long nails. She was our neighborhood's busybody talking shit about everyone, including my mom. My mother was a beautiful woman and the men on the block admired her. But Naomi had a husband, so she thought she was better than the single moms. As her children came around the corner disheveled and crying, Javi screamed, "Aidita hit us." She blocked me and grabbed me by my arm. China made it up the stairs. She scolded me and called me "hija de puta," which means *daughter of a bitch*. I was scared she was going to hit me. The harder she pressed my arm, the louder she became, so she didn't see the green object flying in her direction. It cut the air between us and I cut loose and jumped out of the way. My mother had hurled my brother's Green Machine Big Wheel and it landed on her chest. I joined my brother upstairs and watched from the balcony. My mother had been fighting her entire life, this was an opportunity to blow off some steam. She kicked Naomi's ass like she was her child. I was instantly reminded that my mother loved me. Nobody fucked with her cubs. The police were never called when stuff like that happened unless an ambulance was needed. People would just have their fights until they were tired and went home. It would be the topic of gossip for the next few days and then the next thing would happen and they'd move on.

After that altercation, my mother took us upstairs, fed us, and we took baths. Early that evening she took us back outside to the ice cream truck. Then we ran and played some more—it was like she was rewarding us. My brother rode his Big Wheel back and forth like a mad man with a black eye and chocolate all around his mouth, and I ran alongside him, charging with our victory hands in the air.

Sarnosa

"Puerto Ricans are like pit bulls!" my grandmother said. "We have that mix of blood that can make us go either way: we can be as sweet as the best of them or as vicious as they come. It all depends on how you treat us."

I was raised to be proud to be Puerto Rican (even though half of me is Dominican—I was never encouraged to claim that). I was "pura taína," which meant I was the embodiment of the island's natives, the pure indios of my land, before colonization. My uncles wore the flag proudly. Though they had never been to the island, they had always connected with it, lovingly and proudly. And when I say they wore the flag proudly, I also mean excessively. Indeed, there is something almost witchy about Puerto Rican pride. It was actually against the law in 1948 to display the flag, so my uncle Davie's response to that gag law was a flag on his bike. He had those old-school, knee-high basketball socks in the colors of the flag, he had shirts and pants and pocket squares, it was even tattooed on his body. We are a cult and that is our symbol!

We grew up Puerto Rican in America, listening to Héctor Lavoe and the Fania All Stars, eating arroz con gandules and dragging the r's like they do on the island. Being "Puerto Rican," I had always believed that I was beautiful and perfect. I carried African and native blood and that was truly the best mix in my mind. I loved everything about me, especially my skin tone. I spoke Spanglish and insisted that it was the only language, basking in the glory of being Boricua. Something about innocence, no matter how misinformed—it's almost perfect to be that pure of heart.

My mother was such a damn beautiful young woman that it was hard for any man to stay away. She would walk down the street and all you heard was whistling and catcalling. She was a victim of her own beauty, constantly being objectified and victimized by the toxic men who surrounded her. I wished I could kick all their asses. I would watch Bruce Lee movies with my uncles and practice. One day I was going to fuck everybody up who hurt my mama. A promise that I made to myself as a very little girl and to this day am still trying to fulfill.

The old Cubans in our neighborhood were there before my family arrived. But now there were new Cubans who were coming in and they were met with skepticism and scrutiny. People looked down on them as a narrative was built around them that was insulting and downright awful. Gustavo came in on the Mariel boatlift and settled in Miami for some time. He moved into apartment 6 of the building my grandmother managed. He shared it with five other guys who had also come from Cuba. They were different, loud and colorful. They sat on the balcony drinking beer, shouting, and joking around. They cursed a lot and their profanity was different, words I had never heard before, words like "sapingo" which I am almost sure means "fuckboy." And I thought I had heard them all. If any of them happened to be on the balcony when my mother came home, it was a nightmare. Nonstop catcalling, it was gross. Rape culture was upon us and we didn't even have a name for it. We didn't know that it was wrong, or at least we pretended it wasn't. My mother had to feel uncomfortable, I know I did.

We were doing just fine at the time. It was the three of us and we had peace in our lives. My mom was looking for jobs and my uncle Raymond and grandmother helped out with us. We had a happy mom and I was her personal entertainment. At night when we were home getting ready for bed, I'd pick up the broom and do my Johnny Carson impersonation for her, speaking directly into my mic, "I did not know that." We were fine.

To this day I don't know what it was about him that my mother found attractive. Maybe she had given up and thought this was the best she could do. He was a working man and in our neighborhood that was a big deal. She liked him, although there were others in that apartment who were cuter and not as loud. He screamed a lot, in his excitement, anger, and even just casual conversation. I was afraid of him.

Gustavo pursued my mom, and she liked it. She was twenty-four, he was twenty-five. She was tired of doing it alone and really wanted a father for her children. She was raising us the best she could, but it was hard to make ends meet. You had to have a job to pay a babysitter and needed a babysitter to look for a job. Things were hard. She was a young and lonely woman, and up until now, she hadn't had much luck with men. She was trying to do the right thing for us. She also really liked him. They made each other laugh. He brought her flowers and took her out on dates, while my grandmother watched us. She wanted my mom to find a man, she wanted her daughter to have security. My mom was being courted, that felt new to all of us.

A few dates in, we were scheduled to officially meet him. He was coming over for dinner—it was time to see if we all fit. I really wasn't excited at all, I always felt threatened by any man that came near us. I was afraid for several reasons ranging from being molested again to losing my mother. It was stressful. Plus, I had my little brother to look after now.

Gustavo was very nice when he walked in. He picked my brother up and shook my hand. He was charming and funny. He then tickled my brother and pinched my nose. We were off to a good start. And then my mom asked me to go to the room. I felt as if she was pushing me away. I don't know what came over me, but I called her the devil. Gustavo chuckled hard but it was almost as if he was instigating. She popped me right there in front of him. She said that I was talking out of turn, the children were not supposed to talk when the adults were around. Los niños hablan cuando la gallina mea. Which literally translates to, children speak when hens pee. But she was trying to impress him by showing him that she had control over her kids. She wanted him to know that she was a disciplinarian. He ate it up and continued to laugh, and then inserted his passive-aggressive opinion that I was going to be a problem later in life.

There was this urban myth that Puerto Rican men were lazy womanizers, and that Cubans were hardworking family men. My mom's experiences with Puerto Rican and Dominican men were not good, so she believed it. Gustavo began to press hard and would not go away. As I watched my mom fall in love again, I braced myself for another ride. She really believed he was a good choice. After being with a man who was on the FBI's Most Wanted list, anything was a step up.

I knew that he didn't like me, but I didn't know why. I was just a little girl. He was not very affectionate toward me like he was with my brother, but he wasn't mean. He just kept his distance. The further he pushed away, the more I was away from my mom. My fears were being confirmed. This would be the beginning of me losing my mother again, and my little brother, China, would be all I had left. I had to protect him at all costs.

They moved in together and became an official item. Our family dynamic shifted—he was now in charge of all of us. His charm slowly began to wear off and the yelling became more frequent. My mom became more isolated from everyone and my family stopped visiting us.

He was incredibly controlling; his expectations were extra clear. My mom was a housewife and mother, she cooked, cleaned, and took care of us. She didn't have to work, all she had to do was take care of us. She would go to school and speak to my teachers frequently and had to make sure I did my homework. We had dinner at the table together. But after dinner she would go in the room with him and we would not see her until the next day. This was our new family. What others saw as a major improvement in her life, I saw as total misery. I missed my mom.

About a year in, he took us to meet his aunt and uncle on a Sunday. He had already met our entire family, but we knew none of his. We drove to the other side of town, to a middle-class neighborhood in Southwest Miami where middle-class Cubans lived, the ones who had come in the 1960s and were upwardly mobile.

I felt the cultural difference immediately. I had been around Puerto Rican people my entire life and they were not like us. They sounded different; their Spanish dialect was faster and a bit sharper. Puerto Ricans sang when they spoke, they dragged a little. They were also all the same color. Unlike my family, they were all white. They were nice but they did not feel like family. They didn't treat us like family either.

We ate dinner at their house, their beans were black. I was used to my red ones. Their plantains were sweet, I preferred tostones, the salty ones. They drank Coke with their dinner. My mom and Gustavo's aunt Delia exchanged recipes. She had to learn how to cook these Cuban dishes for her man. From this point forward we would eat those damn black beans every day.

We ate flan for dessert and they continued their conversation while my brother and I enjoyed the sweets. And then I heard what was supposed to be a compliment but felt like a jab. Delia pointed out that I was cute but I would've been perfect if I wasn't so "ordinaria," in other words, if I didn't have Afrocentric features. She was referring to me not having a perfectly keen nose and super thin lips. Even though my mother's lips weren't thin either, she had lighter skin to save her from association with Blackness. She pinched my nose while clearing the plates, I wanted to bite her hand off. She was definitely not nice.

Everything I knew about me was beautiful according to my people, and here was this lady pointing out my flaws. How could my mother let this happen? I had already been struggling with my self-esteem since New York, I didn't need to feel uglier. I had to fight through it and remember what my grandmother told me, I was a "pura taína." That was a good thing.

I looked like my uncle Pedro and he was the most beautiful man I had ever seen. I never thought anything was wrong with him—until now. I knew my father had to be darker than my mom because of my brown complexion. I just looked different. I was tall and my hair was dark. It was here that I began to question everything that I had known about myself and my people. This is when I started hearing all the stereotypes and awful things about Puerto Ricans.

On the ride home from that hellish house, he described my skin tone as being Black. He joked and called me negra. He gave me the nickname "Sarnosa." That was a word I had never heard before, but I knew it was bad. I held on to it until I got to school to find out what it meant. On Monday when I got to school, I asked my Cuban Spanish teacher, Señora Castellano, what the word *sarnosa* meant in English. She was curious about where I had heard it and asked me to share the sentence with the class to make it a teaching moment. Something about the way he said it, "Tú eres sarnosa," made me feel like it was not good and I didn't want to quote him just in case. So I said, "No quiero ser sarnosa," which meant "I don't want to be sarnosa." After class she told me what it meant: "filthy, grimy, dirty." It hurt, she knew that it was personal for me and assured me that I wasn't dirty. I was relieved I didn't say that in class because I was in elementary school and those kids were unforgiving. Although my classmates never knew what that word meant to me and where it came from, I knew and it was surely a warning about the hell that was to come in my life with this man. I was so angry about not having my real father at the time. I thought that the only actual filthy people on the planet were the men my mother chose to be with and that was especially my new stepfather, he was the sarnoso!

I became devoted to language early on. My second-grade teacher, Mrs. Ventura, told me that scoring high on tests was the gateway to college. "That is how to build your word bank and score high on tests." I took that shit to heart; it was a way out and away from these people that were my family. I started to learn more words and weaponize them. And even though I would not vocalize them yet, I was laying the foundation for what would be the future wordsmith in me.

Your Mama Is a Ho!

"Castro flushed the toilets of Cuba and all the shit ended up in Miami," Ruthy, my friend Alba's mom, said with no hesitation. My mom looked on as if she didn't hear it. It was confusing because Ruthy was Cuban.

I was a prepubescent girl who had played mostly with boys my entire life and was eager to find girls to play with now. My mother and my stepfather had a son, my baby brother. I was around them constantly and desperately needed some feminine energy. I met Delai and Bambi, while racing one of the boys on the block. We ran from our side of the street to the other and back. The sisters started cheering in Spanish and invited themselves into our game. They were new on the block, part of the group of people who came during the Mariel boatlift from Cuba.

Unlike any girls I had met before, they were eleven and twelve and spoke like thirty-year-olds. They had come to America on those boats. They cursed up a storm and were loud. Delai was older, blond, with green eyes, and her clothes were very tight. She had on black wing-tip eyeliner that made her eyes pop. Barbara, aka Bambi, was a little different. She looked more like me complexion-wise: her skin was brown, and she had dark hair and eyes. She was thinner and dressed like her sister, but her clothes fit too big. She was the quieter of the two—but still loud. I wasn't allowed to wear pants that short, or makeup, or curse. We could not be more different and I found them fascinating. I was eleven years old, like Bambi, but they felt much older than me.

"¿Cómo te llamas?" *What's your name?*

I responded, "Aidita," and we became instant friends.

I was only allowed to play with them when they came over to our lot. Because they were pretty and flirty, even the boys welcomed them with open arms and all wanted them on their teams regardless of how good they were.

Seeing them move freely, playing, flirting, dancing, doing all the things I wanted to do but wasn't allowed to, I couldn't help but be jealous. They were happy, living their best lives, and I wanted that for myself too.

Meanwhile, the grown-ups were so fucking toxic, they talked about these girls like they were streetwalkers, constantly slut-shaming them. "Son puticas," Margo in our building would say, referring to them as little whores. My God, they were *kids*. Nevertheless, she warned, "Be careful. That shit rubs off." And of course, being a puta always ended in unwanted pregnancy. Not fun to hear when I knew that I was a product of a teenage pregnancy—I was unwanted.

The more they talked about them, the more I gravitated toward them. I liked hanging around them, they made me feel like I was pretty too. I started sneaking over to their house and playing with makeup. On the flip side, I still played with my Barbies, my mom was still picking out my clothes and hairstyles, and I was scared to curse. But I felt like a big girl when I was around them and I brought the little girls out of them. We played kickball, hide-and-seek, and Mother, May I. They never talked about sex or did any of the things others accused them of doing. They liked boys but so did I. I liked boys long before they ever came along, I just kept it to myself. Expressing that would get me in trouble. My mom started to let up a little when she saw that I was having a good time, but someone was always watching. There was never a moment when there wasn't an eye on me. Shit, if I knew that all I needed to do to get some attention was make friends with some "hot girls," I would have done that a long time ago.

Delai was charming, and she knew it. She would play on the team with the boys and they would always let her kick first. I had to work hard for my spot. I learned from them, they taught me how to tap into my femininity and use it to get what I wanted from boys. It didn't work on the boys on my block because they didn't see me that way, but I was definitely getting attention at school. And after hiding from male attention for some time, thinking that if I was too pretty or girly it would bring on something awful, I began to embrace it.

Anyway, we hung out, we played, we had fun. I remember the first time I ever saw their mother, Evilia. She came down the street wearing tight white jeans, cork heel sandals, and a loud yellow tank top exposing her cleavage. She had long, curly hair, wild hair, just like her daughter Delai. Her shoes scraped the ground as she walked, making a scratchy sound. She was loud too. Summers in Miami were hot, sweaty, muggy, and wet. Fresh after a shower, I felt like I needed another one. This lady was impressive, she had it together.

"This is Aidita," the girls said excitedly, introducing me to their mom, and all I smelled was coconut. She looked me up and down, and I could see judgment on her face. I was poor, we couldn't afford expensive clothes. From my understanding, everyone on my block was poor. Why was she looking at me like that? This was the pretty me. What exactly made the three of them better than me? Their lighter skin, the green eyes. Bambi had my complexion. Just when I was beginning to come out of my shell and feel more confident, her one look triggered endless questions of self-doubt. She made me feel bad. I was dealing with colorism at home with my stepfather, and she only helped reinforce the negative things I constantly heard about Cubans.

Was it where I lived? They lived in an apartment too; it was attached to the back of a house. There had been so much talk from the adults about the buildings versus the houses. Was it that she had a job cleaning houses and my mom was unemployed? But she was on assistance and my stepdad barely let my mom leave the house. There was so much dissent and competitiveness. So, who was better? The citizens or the undocumented; the whites, Blacks, or indigenous; the houses or the buildings; the single or married women? Every aspect of our communities seemed to be weaponized to create some sort of hierarchy.

In my eleven-year-old mind, I just wanted to know why my new friends' mom didn't like me. I was coming to life in a new way with their friendship, I finally was someone at school. They had so much to do with me feeling good at the time. What did I need to do to fix this? That was the last time we ever hung out together.

They never came around after that. They even avoided me at school, and I never understood why. I was hurt. I wondered if my mom had done something to the lady. Did she beat her up? Months passed and we grew further and further apart, only occasionally waving at one another from a distance.

A while later, I once again ventured out to play kickball with the boys. Things had returned to the way they used to be: me fighting for my position, never getting to kick first. During one of those super-hot Miami days, when the sun was unrelenting and we refused to quit playing until the ice cream truck came around, dashing for our snacks—sodas, potato chips, and pickles were on deck—we copped a squat on the grass to delight in our favorites. As we devised our plan to play our next game with less players, I told my friend Jose, "I wish Bambi and Delai were here to fill out the spaces." I really missed them.

And then he blurted out, "They can't play with you because your mama is a ho."

The other kids laughed, and I honestly didn't know exactly what that meant, but I was sure it had something to do with being with multiple men. It was no secret that my brothers and I had different fathers. I knew it wasn't good. I didn't like when people talked about my mom. She had been through so much—they didn't know her life. She was a good person and mother, she loved her kids.

In that one moment, every positive feeling I ever had for those girls went immediately down the drain. They were the enemy now and their sorry-ass mother could go to hell. A knot formed in my throat. I was so angry I could've fought them right then and there. Nobody talked about my mama! I had to defend her.

"You know what? My mama is not a ho. My mom is a decent woman that you've never seen wearing tight clothes and looking like a clown. You never see her talking to any men other than my stepfather! That lady is a ho and her daughters are too!"

I took my bag of Doritos and marched home, after having officially joined the slut-shaming committee. I didn't know how to process what I was feeling, so it just turned into judgment and hate. I jumped back in with my Jesus and stopped wearing eyeliner behind my mother's back. I was back to being a good girl.

After that, I quietly declared war against them until they moved away. I now see that the situation was largely the result of my unhealthy views of women and myself. Lord knows those attitudes were incredibly harmful to all of us. They had to deal with so much as well, like being called everything from hoes to refugees. Thank God for deliverance. I think of them often as I have grown and evolved in my views. They had a positive impact on me at such a young age, being confident in their bodies and having agency in how they wanted to present themselves. Little did they know that they were ahead of their time.

The Witness

I lived in a building with ten apartments in it—seven of them housed single moms. I don't remember them, but I do remember the families that had fathers in the homes. I never really thought about that stuff, until I saw it. It was decidedly different from my family. I had a step-father. I saw a difference in how biological fathers treated their own daughters versus how my stepfather treated me. Even in a simple introduction you could see it, one of our neighbors would say, "This is Diana," and you knew that was his daughter. My stepfather, on the other hand, would introduce me as Margarita's daughter, making it very clear that I was not his.

There was something interesting to me about the families with dads—I fixated on them. I would stare from my balcony when I saw them outside, paying attention to their interactions, like how a father would hold his daughter with confidence and no weirdness. At this point I didn't really have any physical interactions with men unless one of my uncles came around. They always hugged and kissed me, that never stopped.

In apartment 7, Mina had two sons and married a man named Sergio, with whom she had another son. Her two older boys would pay the price for anything that went wrong in that house. Sergio was verbally and emotionally abusive, he also beat their asses. By then, I believed that stepfathers were a punishment.

The story was much different in apartment 9. My friend Norma Linda and her brother Santi lived there with both parents. Their place was across from us, they were such a cool family. They were Jehovah's Witnesses and totally in sync. They dressed nice, they were polite and kind. I would watch them go door to door, ministering. People in our building made fun of them. They criticized them for not celebrating birthdays and being against blood transfusions. My mom questioned their parenting for not being willing to do anything to save their children's lives. But I thought they were cool, I wished that I could go with them to Kingdom Hall. My mom's friend Ruthie called them freaks, she was jealous because she couldn't keep a man to help her raise her bad-ass kids.

Norma and her family did a lot of things together. They ate dinner together every night, they played board games and would go on trips. Norma was the first friend I had in the building who called her father "papi." I was so enamored with this family, I spent a lot of time with them. I did my homework there, I ate dinner there, and then we would read the Bible together. This Bible was different from mine but it said the same stuff. They were welcoming, their father was so kind to me. He was respectful, treated me gently, and had no creepy vibes. I was a nine-year-old little girl to him, he had no idea what I had been through. He didn't see me as damaged goods. I felt that way about myself at that point. I had seen a penis, therefore I wasn't pure anymore. But Freddy and his wife, Maria, cared for me, even protected me. When I would leave their apartment at night, they would watch me until I made it inside my place. I was precious to them; that was something I hadn't felt elsewhere. It was cool to be a part of their family in some way. When my mom would come get me, making sure I didn't overstay my welcome, Freddy would always push back, "She's not overstaying her welcome, we love her. She is like another daughter to us."

This didn't sit well with my mom. Feeling threatened, she accused them of trying to convert me into their "weird" religion. Eventually, I wasn't allowed to go over as much. My stepfather referred to them as "indios," which was a slur for Central American indigenous people. Another person in the building, Judith, called our other neighbor from Honduras an Indian. These people were beautiful, they were like us, just from different places. I didn't see that big of a difference. I enjoyed eating different foods and listening to other types of music. Plus, who were these people to talk about Freddy and Maria, the couple who actually had a wedding picture up in their home? They both had jobs and did not receive public assistance, as a matter of fact, they moved in to save up for a house. They were the goal.

For that little bit of time, while my friends lived in the building, I always had a place to go when home wasn't great. Despite my mother's preference, I would still sneak out and head over to their place. I wanted to have a pleasant dinner at a table, I wanted to share my day, and hear their funny stories. The kids went to private school and they went to church a lot as a family, so at home, after school, during dinner was our time.

I turned ten the day they moved away. They saved up enough money to buy that house and relocate to another neighborhood with a better school. It wasn't a big deal to them that they left on my birthday. And I was devastated. That was the worst gift ever. I knew that Norma wouldn't come back. Her mom didn't trust my mom enough to let her even visit my apartment once. Everyone in the building could hear my stepfather yell and curse, people were afraid of him. This was the end of my good dinnertime thing. I was back to my number one buddy, my little brother. The night they pulled off, my mother let me go downstairs to say goodbye. They all gave my brother and me a hug and promised that they would pray for us. There was no mention of a visit, they didn't believe in telling lies. I said goodbye and watched them go with tears streaming down my cheeks. My favorite family was gone. China grabbed my hand and waved with the other. Realizing that I was sad, he then gave me a hug and we went upstairs. That night I played Candy Land with my brother and we started our own game night.

Carlos

The first family trip I remember going on when I was a little kid was with my great-grandfather, Papi; my maternal grandmother, Aida; and my uncle Davie, my mom's youngest brother. I was around eight years old and Uncle Davie was about nineteen. We were going to a part of Florida that was north of Miami. I don't remember the city, but I know that we had to take I-75 North and drive along a two-lane highway that was dangerous for more than being narrow; it also was bordered by two canals that were filled with alligators, hence the name Alligator Alley.

My great-grandfather was in his seventies, young for a great-grandfather, at least I thought so. I don't think I had ever met another great-grandparent at the time. It was a hot, humid Florida day and Papi had on a lot of clothes. He would be the only person in my life that I ever called "Papi," we all called him that. He wore long pants with a T-shirt (that had another T-shirt over it) and a long-sleeved shirt. He would roll his sleeves up and put rubber bands on his forearms to hold the three shirts in place and then fold them over. It was pretty interesting because I always thought that that was probably disrupting his circulation, but he did that every single day.

My uncle Davie and I sat in the back seat with my great-grandfather. My step-grandfather drove and my grandmother sat in the front seat.

Since the driver was in charge of the music, we listened to a radio station that was in Miami called Super Q, a Cuban-run station that played mostly top-of-the-charts Spanish-language songs. My uncle and I sang along—we knew all of them.

The drive along Alligator Alley felt like a safari or going to the zoo. I looked out the window and saw some of the biggest creatures I had never seen before. As it goes, someone always has to use the bathroom on a long trip, and that person was my great-grandfather, who really needed to pee. We pulled over on the freeway so that he could go off to urinate. Of course, he went off by himself because he didn't want anyone to see him do his business. I stood outside of the car stretching my legs, wrestling with my uncle Davie, who was always roughing me up, teaching me to defend myself. If it wasn't practicing karate chops and kicks, it was boxing, it was always something. In the middle of a fake fight, we heard a loud scream and saw my great-grandfather running back up the short hill, pulling his pants up. An alligator spotted him, and he was shaken. But he didn't give us a warning, so as my great-grandfather ran toward us, we ran toward him, instead of all of us running away from the alligator. The funniest part of it all was that when we got to him, he continued to run right past us. As soon as we understood what was going on, we made a quick U-turn and joined him. After jumping back in the car and slamming the doors shut, we sped off. That was the most fun I had in a long time. I was also relieved to be away from home, away from my mom and my stepfather, away from everything that was chaos. I really didn't know where we were going at the time, I just knew that we were going on a family trip and I was happy.

When we finally arrived at our location, I still had no idea what this place was, it was a structure that I had never seen before. There were fences and grass, and a lot of land, as well as a big one-level building that covered a lot of ground. It was a bit overwhelming. We walked in through the first set of gates and were stopped at a guard gate. After my grandmother had a conversation with the man, he looked at a clipboard and allowed us to go past that gate and the next one. Then we walked into another place, an office, and my grandmother had a conversation with someone behind the tall glass window. I remember just putting my arms up and touching what seemed to be some sort of dip you could drop things in, but I couldn't reach its opening. My grandmother slid her ID into that slot and all the other adults followed. I remember them asking, "Is she his daughter?" and my grandmother shaking her head no. We were at a prison in Florida visiting my uncle Carlos.

Uncle Carlos was about twenty-eight years old back then and was serving time in prison for burglary. As I've mentioned, this charming, attractive, six-foot-one man had always been the protector of my family. He was the darkest member of my family, Black and beautiful. To this day I believe that my uncles, serving a paternal role in my family, have a great deal to do with the type of guys that I like, especially physically, because I thought when I was a little girl that my uncles were the handsomest people on the planet. I still do.

Carlos had been locked up for almost a year. Up until then, I had no idea where he had been. They just told me that he was out of town. I would write to him and he would write back, but I never got an envelope. My mom would open and read the letters before she gave them to me. He was my first pen pal. Mrs. Venura, my second-grade teacher, told me that you could have a friend that was on the other side of the world and create a bond by writing about where each person lived. I had been doing that with my uncle Carlos, but only on this day did I learn that he was actually away in prison. This is where my love for writing began, using words to express myself without rebuttal. I would share with my uncle things that I knew I could in confidence. I wrote to him telling him about how

I was zipping through the grocery store with my grandmother and rammed the shopping cart into her right ankle. My grandmother cursed me out in every aisle of the store, she called me a "cabrona" and for some reason I found that hilarious. It was also funny to him because he wrote back telling me he couldn't stop laughing. He also shared that she called him that a couple of times too. I felt very connected to him and he appreciated it. I would tell him about what was going on at school and with my friends. I would skip the home stuff, too scared to tell him about my stepfather. I didn't want him to beat him up—he definitely would have and that would've gotten him in even more trouble. He'd tell me about his days without ever telling me about prison life. He shared the names of different flowers and trees that he learned, and he sent me stories from the Bible. We would exchange thoughts on them and he always encouraged me to do things according to the Word. On my birthday, he sent me a letter and drew a cake in the middle of the page. It had six candles on it, I was eight. He had lost track while being in there. I treasured that letter; it was the only thing that I received on that birthday. I've loved cards ever since. Gifts fade, but words are forever.

Uncle Carlos started doing drugs when he was nine. He couldn't cope with the pain of being in a house where his mother was suffering physical abuse and his sister was being sexually assaulted. Being the eldest boy and carrying the burden of having to be the protector of the family—which is how we always defined him, the tough guy, the bad guy—had to be a lot, especially while he was still a kid. A lot of people turn to drugs because they have pain and they have to self-medicate so that they can cope—because the other option could be much darker. As a result of his addiction, there was a life of crime. It was odd because he was one of the best people I ever met in my life. I knew nothing of this side of him.

We went to visit him that day and it was weird because I wasn't allowed to hug my uncle that much. We had a physical contact visit where we did take a picture together, a picture that I still have in my possession. We were able to just be with him. I'll never forget that day because when I had to leave and they closed the second gate, my uncle was standing behind it. I just remember crying so much because I didn't want to leave him. For some reason, I felt that leaving him behind meant leaving him in a place where he wasn't safe. I could look at his face and know that as much as he smiled and tried to reassure my grandmother that he was fine, he wasn't. I knew that he didn't belong there. I'm sure that many people feel that way about their loved ones. But I was right because four years later my uncle Carlos would die of a blood infection that eventually caused a blood clot to form in his brain and erupt. He never got the help he should have received. He left two beautiful children behind.

My uncle had gotten married when he was just seventeen years old to Lillian, his stepfather's sister, technically his step-aunt. But they met before my grandmother met her husband. They dated, eventually got married, and had a daughter. My uncle and I were very close, so he would talk to me about these things. I knew he loved his daughter deeply because he would always say, "You have a cousin, my first baby girl. I love you both very much, you both are my little girls and I will always protect you."

His relationship was complicated because he was on drugs and his wife was religious. He was the son of the woman that was about to marry her brother and her family didn't think that it was a good idea for them to be together. His marriage eventually ended in divorce and after that, my entire family moved from Boston to Miami. I was still a baby and on my way to the Dominican Republic with my parents at the time.

It was hard for him to not be near his daughter, but he couldn't afford the trips. Lacking the education on how to cope, he turned to drugs to numb the pain. People in our family would say, "Well, why didn't he just get a job and stop?" Those of us who've been raised by addiction and around it know that it is an illness and it takes over your mind and body. It's not that easy. Yes, you have to make the decision to want to have a better life, but you have to believe that you're worth it. I don't know if that was the case when it came to my uncle Carlos.

In time, he got into another relationship and had the son he always wanted, the one whose name he had highlighted in his Bible the day he died. He couldn't show up for him either. It was painful to watch because I knew how much he loved his kids and how he felt he failed them. He would talk to me about it and it made me wonder if my father was somewhere on another side of the world feeling the same.

My first trip out of town was to visit my uncle in prison, but it was a highlight in my life. I loved my uncle so much. I was so young that I didn't understand his circumstances fully. I was just happy to see him. I will never forget how happy he was to see me. I choose that as my preferred memory because he was sober and it was one of the very few times he looked happy. That trek along Alligator Alley was good, if only just for that.

El Día del Pavo

Not having your father means you have to tolerate all of your mother's bullshit. So many times my mom did things to me that I knew a father would have intercepted. My mother was a young mom and she did a lot of things wrong. She didn't know better; there was a lot of trauma there. There was a baby before me that didn't make it, and his father passed away in a game of Russian roulette. She was seventeen and I was her second child. She was angry and misguided and took plenty out on me and if my grandmother or uncles were not around, there was no one to rescue me.

One Thanksgiving morning, when I was in sixth grade, my mother was preparing her meal. Even though my grandmother did most of the cooking and we would always go to her place, Margarita would always make her own Thanksgiving dishes. Mainly because my stepfather wanted traditional Cuban food every day—and this holiday was no exception. She also made some staples to compliment my abuela's meal. My family ate the classic Puerto Rican arroz con gandules, pernil, and the fixings. There was also a pavo-chon, a turkey made pork style. All I knew was that it was delicious. Margarita was a great cook and on the holidays, she would really show out—you could smell her food throughout the building. This was one of her great attributes, according to my stepfather: a real woman should be able to cook and clean the house. My mom did both and was even a bit excessive with the cleaning. She had OCD. She covered every corner of our place, even the crevices of the bathroom, with a toothbrush and bleach. So much cleaning that the doctor said she had a stain on her lung from inhaling so many cleaning agents. It was very important to her to keep a clean house, though. She was trying to dispel the myth that Puerto Rican women were dirty—a Caribbean stereotype generated by the other cultures and constantly reinforced by this man. So we had a clean house, all the time. It was a hard home to play in, have friends visit, just plain live in. We couldn't touch the walls, there could not be a dish in the sink, there was no extra movement. My mother cleaned our room, she organized our closets, everything was neat. She wanted to impress this man so much, she worked daily to please him. And every day he moved the goalposts because he was an asshole.

Before we were able to go to Abuela's, Mami decided to clean the apartment because it was Turkey Day. She liked to clean on special occasions (or, well, on any other occasion really). I think she wanted the entire building to smell her cooking and Pine-Sol. When the women in the building discussed who held the title of "the cleanest woman in the building," of course, my mom was always at the top of her own list.

On this Turkey Day I remember several noises in the background. Salsa music always played. It was either Héctor Lavoe, El Gran Combo, Frankie Ruiz, or any of the 1970s greats. The rice cooker clicked to signal it was done and the hissing sound of the pressure cooker meant the black beans were on the way. I could also hear my mom sweep the floor, that meant that mopping would soon follow. I hated when she mopped because it meant that everyone else had to freeze until the floor dried. Whenever she cleaned, I was confined to either the bedroom, living room couch, balcony, or outside, if I was allowed to go. On this day I decided to stay in the room to watch television. My little brother played his video game on the bed as well. Being off from school was tough, it meant we had to be home.

My mom would sing as she started her weekly routine of la limpieza. This was her happy place. The artificial pine smell was in the air and it was a for sure indicator that she was in her zone. You could hear her put the mop into the bucket and squeeze the water all out and then it would hit the floor with a slap. It was cathartic for her. She was in complete control of everything and everyone. The place was still and she could sing her heart out, doing one of the things she was confident she was good at. I have to admit that it was kind of cool to hear her be joyful and see her dancing around with her mop. She had a method, a technique at times, and she would talk me through it between her favorite songs. "You start at the front of the apartment in the kitchen, then work your way to the living room, by the time you get to the first bedroom, the kitchen is dry. When you are done with the two rooms, you go back and start again. You can't just do it one time, the first time is to clean, the second time is to shine." She was talking to me, not my brother. My brother didn't have to listen, since he would never be expected to know how to clean a house.

As routine would have it, she made her way into my room for the first round that Thanksgiving. She swabbed the entire room, even underneath my bed. "I'll tell you when it's dry," she reminded me, and danced her way back to the entrance of our apartment so that she could start again. I heard her, like I had several times before, but there was one problem this time: I had to pee. No matter where I sat on that bed the feeling would not go away. No jumping, shaking, rolling could ease the need. I was a little kid, and when little kids have to go to the bathroom, they have to go. So I drummed up the courage to say, "Mami, I have to go!" And she yelled back, "Espera que se seque el piso." *Wait for the floor to dry*. That damn floor mattered more than me. But my bladder was full to that point where I could feel my stomach become upset and a burning sensation. By then, I either went in the proper place or I went on myself—there was no holding it anymore. I had to make a decision! If I could just hop over to the bathroom quickly, she would never know. So I made an executive decision and went for it. I made it to the bathroom, relieved myself, and made it back in time before she rolled around the corner with her wooden stick and towel.

Ever since my mom had gotten with my stepfather many things had changed, even her mop. She now used a Cuban mop, and it was making its way into my room. As she entered, she stopped—and so did my heart. She saw my footsteps on the floor and became enraged. "Didn't I tell you to wait for the floor to dry?!" she yelled loudly enough for the entire building to hear. She grabbed that stick she was cleaning the floor with and popped me on my right ankle. It hurt so bad I let out a scream but then she followed up with the infamous "Shut up before I give you something to cry about" and I had to suck it up. That day, she sprained my ankle and I had to go back to school with a limp and a lie. I was not to tell my teacher what had happened or there would be more consequences. The mop that I used as a microphone became the weapon she used to cause the most physical pain I had ever felt.

Where the fuck was my father? I needed him to come defend me. If he had been around, this never would have happened. I started to hurt and hate, taking turns between sobbing for him and cursing him. I cried myself to sleep that night asking God where my father was. I never used that mop to entertain my mother again.

Istata and Pachew

I cut my sister's umbilical cord the day she was born, I had one of the worst migraines of my life. At fourteen years old, watching my mom give birth was definitely not on my bingo card. I had to do it. Gustavo had missed work several times for this. It was supposed to be me.

My siblings and I were always a revolutionary act, we were a visual aid for colorism in our family. We looked different and that made several statements. I was the brown one, my brother looked Asian, and the two babies were white. It meant we had different fathers and there was a hierarchy. We were weaponized against each other when the adults would fight, it never landed on us.

Miami was experiencing many changes; the Cubans, Dominicans, and Puerto Ricans had very different social dynamics. And as similar as we all were, the politics made us different because we all had different journeys. Puerto Ricans were citizens, Dominicans were undocumented, and Cubans sought asylum. My siblings and I were at the intersection of all of that. Our complexions and hair textures could be used against us or in our favor. It was a mess. Our Puerto Rican mother landed in the middle of it all, we were her children. I was half Dominican, China was full-blooded Puerto Rican, and the babies were half Cuban. To her we were just her kids, she was home base, we were what she was. No matter how much my grandmother and stepfather fought and pointed out the differences in us, she continued to remind us that we were all the same. She would pat her vagina: "You all came from here, you are full brothers and sisters as far as I'm concerned." I felt that way too. I adored my siblings.

My mom was happy during her next pregnancy, she was beautiful and glowing. She was happy to have this baby. Her relationship with Gustavo wasn't perfect but he was there. He didn't smoke, drink, or party. That alone was a win. When my baby brother came along, China and I couldn't be happier. I would kiss him and he would laugh, he was such a sweet baby. My stepfather would hoard him, but we always managed to get a hold of him. I was happy he was here; we had another soldier on the squad. I was older and into my girly things, so now China would have someone to do the block with. He needed someone to play with, that was into the things that he was into. I was into boys, eyeliner, and Michael Jackson. I wanted to talk on the phone and watch music videos, because going outside wasn't as fun anymore. It was too hot and I didn't want to get dirty. He came along at just the right time.

My mom had nicknames for all of us. As I've mentioned, I was Aidita and Chino was her China. Now this baby was "Ista-ta," basically the first words that flew out of his mouth. No matter how much they tried to divide us, they couldn't. We were a force, I wasn't going to let anyone interrupt that. I fed my brothers and bathed them. We watched TV together and played in the house. I would get in the way of the belt when they were being punished, I didn't like for them to get hit. As I got older, they got closer. We had our sibling rivalries, of course, but nothing ever lasted long. The busier I became, the more they hung together. They started playing sports and martial arts, they were little active boys that no longer wanted to play with their sister.

When my baby sister came along, so much had changed. I was becoming a teenager and very active in school. I had an afterschool job and was never home. I wanted to go to college, so I knew I had to be active in extracurricular activities to make that happen. I was working to take care of myself and buy what I needed. But when Pachew came along, everything changed again. I was the first person to lay eyes on her, and I almost fainted. I stood in the delivery room facing off with my mother's insides while my head was pounding as my mother screamed at the top of her lungs. My almost ten-pound sister would not be denied, she busted through and I almost hit the floor. The nurse who caught me gave me a chair and a pill. I needed a bed. I had not slept the entire night before while my mother was in labor. But I was the first to see my baby sister and to hold her—she instantly felt mine. I couldn't believe what I had seen and still the first time she cried, I forgot all about it.

Every day after school, I came home to check on my sister. I fed her, changed her diaper, and rocked and sang her to sleep. She was mine and no one could take her away from me.

My family was very divided at this point. Gustavo began to protest my uncles coming around. He said that they were bad influences on us. He and my grandmother hated each other, so she would barely come over. But ultimately, it was us who felt the changes. My grandmother wasn't as close to my other siblings. My mother took care of my younger siblings differently, she was more involved with them. Their father was around, they seemed more like a unit. China was a part of it, I wasn't. He was young enough to be his and he also looked more like him. I stood out, it was obvious that I wasn't his. I didn't even look like my mom.

The adults took their hate for one another out on us and we just wanted to be loved by all of them. Whenever we got together, which was rare now, there was always bickering. Arguments about who was better, who had better hair, who had citizenship, and any ignorant argument possible. There was so much fighting and profanity around us that my baby sister picked it up. One day she just yelled out,

"Pachew!" She heard "fuck you" so much, she was bound to repeat it. Everyone laughed, it broke the ice. We had a good moment until the next bad one. She was three and had said her first bad word. I knew right there and then that my baby sis was going to be a fighter, she was going to be alright.

Fuck the Law, Break the Kids

Growing up in the hood had lots of perks. I remember doing so many things that would be incomprehensible to some of my friends who grew up in one of those safe, functional, balanced places. Food stamps were something that was common currency between those in my habitat, even though it was an embarrassment, a cause for being shamed, it was also as familiar as curtains in the back of an old Puerto Rican man's Fleetwood Cadillac. I remember handling many transactions for the grown-ups that had to do with them.

I would exchange money for the stamps for my mom. She would do this with Lydia in apartment 4, a six-foot Cuban ex-con who was kinda my best friend at the time. Lydia was the black sheep of her family, though not Black at all, in fact probably one of the whitest people I ever knew who spoke Spanish. She was enormous in stature and in presence with bleached blond hair, the thickest jet-black liquid eyeliner, and she always wore stretch pants. One of the things I remember the most is that she always smelled good, she rocked her Avon Imari like it was Chanel No. 5. She was the single mom of two that could not stay out of jail or trouble but would always make it just in time to rescue me from my abusive stepfather. I believe the last time she got busted it was for stealing meat in her baby stroller (yes, with the baby in it) at La Mia, a local grocery store where the Dominicans in our neighborhood loitered outside with their herringbone gold chains and Don Johnson, Miami Vice shoes.

Lydia was known for crime. She did everything from stealing people's welfare checks, selling cocaine, running numbers to major shoplifting. I hated when the first of the month would land on a Saturday because I would have to stand guard and watch for this woman who was my buddy. I never wanted to tell on her. She did lots of wrong, but much of it benefited me and that made me feel special. I loved her, I think even more than her son Luis, or I'm sure I liked her more. She was my friend, she would shoplift my school clothes so that I wouldn't look ridiculous with super short high-water pants and polyester—I hated polyester.

Lydia's parents, Romana and Tico, lived across the street in my grandmother's building (the good one) in apartment 6, raising her son. Luis was a good kid, he looked like a young Bill Hader with really big feet. His grandparents truly loved and took great care of him. He was their pride and joy and the best kid on "la cuadra" according to them. His grandparents were the ringleaders of a nightly roundup where the neighborhood old people sat in a circle, coupled up, and spread gossip and judgment like cream cheese on a bagel. Nobody wanted to end up on that agenda, they declared the neighborhood hoes, thieves, criminals, and bad kids, pretending not to know that their own daughter was at the top of all those lists. They were white Cubans who loved to point out the African Black blood in people. I am sure they discussed me when my grandmother was not around because they knew she didn't play when it came to me. If they fucked around, they'd get evicted.

So, even though I thought she was pretty awesome, Lydia was

their greatest disappointment. Not only did she get me school clothes but she would also check my stepfather whenever he was verbally abusive. Deep down inside, I know my stepfather was afraid of her because she was relentlessly reckless and not scared of anyone, not even the police. She was one of my heroes. Lydia made me want to go to school and be better so that I could get out of the neighborhood. She had a soft spot for my brother China and me, so she would trade cash for food stamps with my mom mainly for us, because she knew it was rough.

My last encounter with food stamps, though, could've landed my friends and me in jail, really. My friend's aunt sent us to the corner store to buy her liquor with the stamps. I believe we broke several laws with that one. Minors buying alcohol with food stamps, sounds like jail and foster care all rolled up in one.

Selena was a modern-day madam from Nicaragua with toasted caramel skin and one shiny gold tooth that was front and center, which she was proud to show off. Her brothel was a little different. She had four daughters ages five to sixteen and was constantly trying to pair them up with men with money, except the little one—not yet. But she definitely was pushing the older ones in the negotiable direction. Her eldest was in high school and involved with Miller, an older (like in his late thirties), "no good" man who happened to be Haitian and obviously enjoyed banging teenage girls. The only thing we had in common was that none of us had our fathers. And even though I thought my situation was bad, there was always someone who had it worse—this was it. If my mother knew that I was hanging out over there, she would've beat my ass with an extension cord.

Selena was incredibly forceful. She would put you in the mindset of one of the ladies in *Brewster Place*. She didn't ask, she told you what to do. I am just not sure she was a good one. Selena would hold court with the West Indian men of her village. There were things you instantly knew by just looking at her. No matter how much she drank, she was never not on her toes, and you knew that whether on her person or in her kitchen drawer, somewhere near was a gun.

When we stopped by to hang out with Nakia, her eldest, Selena would assign chores to us, doing what she did best: putting young girls to work. We had to walk over to the liquor store (in the heart of Liberty City, Miami, one of the two most dangerous, infamous neighborhoods in our inner city) to buy her beer with food stamps. Yeah, we did that. Nothing but jokes on the way there. There were cracks going back and forth. We were oblivious to what was going on outside of our circle, having too much fun, listening to each other make humor out of our misery. We knew that we were not alone in our poverty, stress, and hunger. As we turned the corner to reach Sam's Liquor Market, we heard that one sound a cop car makes that says, "I'm watching you," and it broke us up. We immediately ran into the store, unaware that it made us look even more suspicious.

A man and woman cop walked into the store. For some reason it looked like they were walking slowly. Every time cops were around, it seemed like they were going to stay forever. And they always made you feel like you did something wrong, even if you didn't. The cops were not the good guys in our neighborhoods, they were the reason part of our neighborhoods were burned down. We had riots after unarmed men were wrongfully killed. When something was wrong, they were the last resort. It was always uneasy to be in their presence.

The male cop asked us what we were doing, we answered with the truth, we were running an errand for our adults. The woman just looked at us suspiciously, but you could tell she was just being facetious. Yet for some reason the guy behind the register was cool. He wasn't moved in any way. They bought two beers like they weren't on duty and wearing those fear-provoking uniforms. Budweiser at that—yes, I was judging. The cops, the man behind the counter, and Selena's kids were all in on it, and I was the odd one out. It scared me so much that I never went back over there. That was unnecessary trauma.

What's for Lunch?

My first memory of liking a boy is when I was eight and in the third grade. His name was Andres Colon and he was very cute. He looked like my uncles and I remember thinking he belonged to my tribe— even though I had no idea what a tribe was. He also looked like me. We had the same complexion, hair color, and were both tall for our ages. He was Puerto Rican and Cuban, and also grew up in the same type of neighborhood as my own, which was half Latino and half Black American. He had a friend group that looked like mine. He spoke like me. He was also fluent in English and in Spanish, had a mom who was fluent in English, and siblings who were fluent in English. He lived in a building just like mine, which made me feel comfortable because when I was a kid, I thought living in a house was scary. I guess every scary movie that I had seen was associated with a house and not a building. So for some reason, at that age, I believed that a building was safer—I actually continued to believe that for a long time.

Now, in terms of personality, Andres was the opposite of me. He was extremely quiet, so he and I barely spoke as kids other than the occasional hi. I had a crush on him on and off up until high school. But throughout elementary school, he was a little bit more advanced than I was. He was out in the street doing things. I don't know what those things were, but I heard he was up to no good, so I assumed that they had to do with being around people who sold drugs and committed crimes, just for the sake of survival—in other words, being around people who were not like my friends, who were still playing hopscotch and jacks, and even with Barbies, because I had Barbies up until I was a freshman in high school.

I was not allowed to have a boyfriend until I graduated high school because, as I was told, boyfriends ruin the lives of young girls—because, of course, young women didn't have any agency. Men were always the villains in our lives, even though we volunteered for many things that happened to us. Being able to blame them just felt a lot easier because they had more power.

So I became a bookworm, and everyone began calling me a nerd. Between fourth and sixth grade, I had some of the best teachers. Those women inspired me and filled me with positive reinforcement when it came to education—I was constantly being told I was highly intelligent, beautiful, and a good person—which was essential in the steps I'd take later in my life. They made a powerful impression on me and made me want to do better in life and be better. I even went on to take honors classes when I was in junior high school. What I wasn't getting at home, I was getting from these teachers at school and I'm forever grateful for that.

But when I got to high school and I blossomed, things changed with Andres. With time, he and I became friends and we started talking on the phone. Then, we developed a relationship of sorts, I guess—whatever relationship you have when you're that young. I learned that Andres was actually on house arrest because he had driven a car that was involved in a crime and they couldn't connect him in the act, but they did connect him to the crime and therefore there were some charges. I remember visiting him and talking, but there was no real physical contact. There was really nothing going on. I don't think I was ready mentally to try to be involved in any type of physical relationship. I was quite squeamish and still scared at the time.

When my mom found out I was spending time with him, she beat the shit out of me with only one message: *stay away from him, he is bad news.* Of course, when you are told to stay away from something at that age, you want it even more. I didn't know any better, so I started sneaking around school and going to his house when my mother thought I was at work. I tried to spend as much time as I could with him. Funnily enough, I can't really say that I liked him that much. He and I didn't have much in common outside of music—I was a nerd that loved school and he couldn't wait to be done with it. I think I was just rebelling against my mom, facing off with her, behind her back, of course. If she thought some boy could derail me, she didn't know who I was. I was strong and smart and wasn't going to let that happen to me.

While Andres was with me, he was also involved with another girl and she found out about us. Not just that, she had a baby with him and apparently thought they were still in a relationship. Who could blame her? She was seventeen and a freshman with a child. I felt sorry for her, I didn't hate her. But I became the mortal enemy and she started bullying me at school, following me to my classes, cursing me out and threatening me. At first, I ignored her because I didn't know what to do. I wasn't much of a fighter back then. I was just trying to get to college so that I could get out of that neighborhood and never have to see any of those people again. I did what I saw in any John Hughes's movie, I took the high road and moved forward with my life because I had one.

Then came the threat that I could not ignore. She had had a conversation with Andres and apparently, he stood up for me and told her to leave me alone and that infuriated her more. She sent a message that she was going to beat me and my best friend up and was going to stab us. I was so scared I told my friend Ellis, who was technically my first "boyfriend,"—it was short-lived, I thought we were better as friends, and I was right; we're still friends today. He became my confidant and never told anyone anything that I told him, he was a vault. But my best friend, Elora, and I were seriously worried. As my ride or die, she somehow got pulled into the drama by association, and she never backed down from anything that had to do with me. We did everything together: we took classes together, were in speech and debate together, we even worked at the same place. The threat that was mine was also hers and she was not afraid to stand up to it, although I knew she wasn't really excited about fighting. We weren't those kids, we just wanted to go to college and get good jobs.

On the day of said fight, we were petrified. I didn't want to be involved in anything that could set me back or deter me from my path of getting out of my neighborhood. I was also exhausted from fighting my whole life, even if that life was not even that long yet. I had to fight my way through school, I had to deal with my step-father, fight at home. Even on my way to school, during those dark morning hours before the sun came up, I had to fight off some predator on the way to school. Men would stick out their tongues and catcall me, trying to lure me into alleys. It was like an obstacle course just getting to school, always carrying the fear of something happening to you on the way there. That morning, I was followed by some man in a van who pulled up to me, exposed himself, and sprinted off. I ran through a church parking lot that led me to the main intersection. Once I crossed, I knew I was safe because it was part of my morning routine. I was always running, fearing that I was going to get assaulted. My route let right out on the football field during morning practice.

That morning I was extra tired because I had worked the night before. My job at the Foot Locker would sometimes keep me until ten at night and then I had to catch the bus home, go to sleep, and wake up before dawn to face the new day's fears. To think that at lunchtime, about five hours after getting to school, I would have to fight felt like an additional burden along with everything else that was going on. I didn't want to fight, but maybe it wouldn't be so bad. After all, I now had someone to take out all that rage on. I mean, here I was, almost at the finish line, and this girl was trying to take it all away from me. I was furious about that, it made me develop feelings of hate for her. I daydreamed about bad things happening to her just to get her out of my way. But I wasn't so lucky.

I walked from one class to the next that morning, wishing those first three periods before lunch would stretch out in time. But of course, when you know that something bad is going to happen, for some reason time just speeds up. My best girl and I met up after our third period and decided to confront the situation head on. There was really no way out of it. Everyone knew about it at this point, and these girls had to save face—we knew they were not going to leave us alone. They also came from broken homes and bad situations and for some reason thought we had it better than them. We were seen as having a better life because we were in the special programs and honors classes. At least that was better than their situation. I understand it now, but back then I just hated them and thought they were mean, evil, and jealous girls who were upset with us because we were pretty and had a future. We just didn't understand their circumstances and they didn't understand ours. Now, looking back, I get that we were all doing bad and were just doing the best we could to survive.

Elora and I discussed a combat strategy, removed our jewelry, and braced ourselves to go outside for lunch, reluctantly pressing forward. If we didn't show up, we would've been called "chickens" or "scary" and made fun of for not standing up to the fight. That would then turn us into the target of other bullies, so we knew we just had to throw down. We talked about telling somebody, but that would've made us snitches, which would've made us even more vulnerable to other people. It was time to face our fears and prepare ourselves for a beatdown, at least we would go down fighting.

Our normal lunch spot was La Havana, a Cuban sandwich shop

in the middle of Allapattah on Seventeenth Avenue, just two blocks away from our school, a straight shot. We would cross the street, walk a little over a block, and reach the sandwich shop on the right. Orders were taken from a window facing the street. There was always a line because it had the best sandwiches. After we grabbed our lunch, we'd usually walk back to school to eat on campus. That was the plan on this day too. Even if there was a fight between school and the sandwich, we prepared ourselves for that.

As we crossed the street and walked into the intersection, we could see the girls gathering, preparing themselves for us to get to the other side. We strolled through the intersection and headed into the battlefield, feeling the girls coming on. And just as they headed for us, a car going at full speed pulled up with a loud screech practically on the sidewalk and everything came to a standstill. We were so caught up in the moment we didn't realize it was our friend Ellis. Then out jumped my mother swinging a bat in the direction of these girls. And they started to back away. All I remember was her screaming, "I know all of you don't have a future and you're mad and jealous of these girls. But if anybody's going to fight, it's going to be me. If you guys want to fight somebody, let's go. Because if you lay a hand on her, I'm going to beat the shit out of every single one of you with this bat, and I guarantee you that I will win. I've been doing this a lot longer than all of you." The girls scattered and ran.

I got to tell you, as embarrassed as I was, relief washed over me. It felt pretty good to have someone defend you and your honor in that way, I was so glad my mom did that. My best friend and I burst out laughing and headed back to our regular lunch spot to eat our sandwiches. Meanwhile, my mother got back in the car, drove to the school, had a conversation with the principal, and had the girls suspended for carrying weapons to school. Even though we knew there would be some social consequences to deal with because my mom showed up, it was okay, we were almost at the finish line.

The hardest part about the whole situation was Andres. He was furious with me because he thought I told my mother. He thought

I had betrayed him. He felt that she bullied the girls without taking into account what I had been going through at the hands of his baby's mama. That's where he lost me. He thought it was an unfair fight that my mother would show up with a bat to stand up to six girls who had knives and were going to use them to hurt my best friend and me, but didn't think it was an unfair fight that a gang was going to assault two girls with knives and beat them to a pulp because of him.

Needless to say, he and I stopped being friends that day. I eventually met someone else who was better for me, a boy who loved school and dreamed about moving beyond those walls, just like me. Losing Andres was actually a gain for me because he was not the person I needed to be around while I was aspiring to be a better version of myself. Third to ninth grade was a fantasy in my head, but in real life, I was actually being saved from being in something that could have very much got me hurt and ruined where I wanted to go in life. All of that went down in one day, and all I could think about was the delicious sandwich I had in my hands.

PART II

Metamorphosis

The Great Debater

I was walking across the street on Florida State University's campus, minding my own business, as a car pulled up too closely for my comfort. I was there for a summer enrichment program that targeted kids from disadvantaged backgrounds to prepare them for college. The driver of the car was one of my former counselors in the program, Dee. He played too much. On the passenger side was this guy whom I couldn't see that well. I did notice his super thick eyebrows, nice smile, very dark, smooth skin. As I looked closer, he reminded me of sports commentator Ahmad Rashad. Dee introduced me to this guy, "This is Aida." The guy says to me, "How are you doing?" And with my dry "I'm good," I kept it moving.

Later that night, I ran into Dee at our student union for dinner and he said to me, "Hey, my friend Dillan told me that you are his future wife." I hit back, "Never! I can't walk around with kids that look like raccoons, he needs to get those eyebrows waxed." I dumped my tray and headed out. I could hear Dee's laugh all the way out the door. The next time I saw "Eyebrows" he was all teeth, but he was so cute. Still, I wanted to stay focused on my mission to become the first person in my family to go to college. This program was intense. We were getting a year's curriculum in one week, I couldn't afford to play. I said hi and moved along. The attraction was definitely there, so I knew any conversation could potentially be trouble.

But of course that's not the way it works. I started to see him more, ran into him in places that I never had before. I saw something I liked and I wanted to know more, and all of a sudden he was around to feed my curiosities. It started with a simple hello and ended in an exchange of phone numbers in the dorm lobby. I wanted to talk to him. The first time we spoke on the phone I expressed my desire for a grape soda from the vending machine in our basement. I was scared to go down there at night—the dark was never where I wanted to go. He put me on hold and shortly after there was a knock on my door. When I opened, the soda was sitting on the floor. I thanked him as I sipped on my drink and he refused to take credit for it. He insisted that there was a hobbit running around the campus doing good deeds. That was our first real laugh.

Over the next couple of weeks, as we tried to get to know each other a little better, I started to not like this guy. We didn't get along, we had very differing points of views on many things, one being the roles of women. As a third generation Sunni Muslim, he had a very traditional take on things. I had been Seventh-day Adventist up until this point, and both religions had similar views about women. I was opposed to them both. According to both faiths, women should dress modestly and take a secondary role in relationships. He told me that women should only look the men they were with in the eye—no other men. No hugging or touching other males was acceptable and, if we married, I was probably going to be at home. That was a direct conflict with who I was and, more important, what I was working on becoming. Law school, writing, communications, modeling were all possibilities in my head and they required me to look a certain way and interact with others, including males. I pushed back and constantly reinforced my views and he would laugh it off, like he would convince me otherwise. He thought that it was funny and would call me feisty. I thought him being so narrow-minded and pig-headed was annoying. Our conversations were heated and intense and challenging. He made me think so much that I would prepare for our next debate. It was a real love-hate thing.

We had some classes together and would see each other in the lobby of my dorm. Our group listened to music and partied as much as we could for kids that had strict rules and a curfew. Sometimes we just sat around the lobby kickin' it.

Our next interaction was sparked one night while listening to 2 Live Crew, a hip-hop group from my city that had defied all the rules—they even fought obscenity charges in a federal appeals court and won. There was something about the power they exuded when they used their words on the microphone. I wanted that. I had something to say, I was very opinionated at fourteen. They fought against Tipper Gore's censorship and gave our ghetto a voice. But I was conflicted about the music. I enjoyed dancing to it but I couldn't help but hear the lyrics and cringe. I had thoughts about that, and how we little girls from the inner city felt about what they were saying. I wanted us to have power and agency. If we were raunchy, it was because we wanted to be.

We went from some dancing to a full-on spirited conversation about the music and it polarized the room. It was suddenly the girls versus the guys, with the exception of a few who saw it another way—of course there were some self-hating girls who would always side with the males on women versus men issues to get their validation and approval. Then there were the fully liberated girls who loved everything about sex. I believed the music was harmful for women and I stood up and said it. I went on a rant about misogyny and machismo that was abruptly interrupted by the lyrics "Nibble on my dick like a rat does cheese." He had gone to his dorm and grabbed his boom box while I was talking and responded with his favorite song. The debate got heated, the room split, and we were in full motion. We were both serving up good points, our audience of classmates responded with aahs and ohs. I was intrigued by the fact that someone who believed women should be modest and demure could easily be in support of porn in the form of a song, and I said as much. He ignored me and focused on the men's freedom of speech rights. That was when I realized that it had nothing to do with the women. He wasn't even thinking about them. They were simply objects. He couldn't care less about their objectification because they didn't matter to him and that made me hate him. I was so upset that I walked out of the lobby and went straight to my room. I was done. I paced, screamed, and then decided to write. I had to do something. I felt it was my duty. I had been an object before and I knew what it felt like to be reduced to just that. I knew the anguish of someone being able to do something awful to you and not having to deal with any consequences. I felt this music was exploitive in that way. There needed to be consequences.

I sat and wrote in my journal, and my phone rang. I ignored it, I didn't really want to talk to anyone, but it wouldn't stop. I finally got up and answered and it was him. I couldn't believe he was calling me. He was the last person I wanted to talk to. But I liked him and the fact that he could make me so mad made it obvious to me. I was so angry with him because I wanted to believe that he saw me as an equal and a human and that I mattered. That was exactly what I told him. I explained that it was important for me to be heard and respected and I couldn't be around anyone who didn't do that. Surprisingly, he agreed. He told me that he just wanted to win the debate. I didn't know that people saw me as smart and a leader, but he brought it to my attention. He was a Black football player, that's all some people saw, and he wanted to be more. So he decided that if he could take on the smart and well-spoken debater girl who was lauded by her classmates, he could earn some respect and be seen as more than just a dumb jock. And just like that, he got me again. We talked for hours and laughed. He was so smart and I couldn't understand why anyone would doubt it. I met him outside for a walk later that night and he asked me to be his girlfriend. I said yes. We were inseparable from that moment on.

He was my first official boyfriend, recognized by the higher court that was my family. I had a few "play, play" boyfriends, as they would call them on the block. Boys that held your hand and carried your books, the ones you went to lunch with and dressed alike with. But you wouldn't have any sexual contact with, no necking, petting, or touching. Maybe innocent kissing but nothing that could really lead to sex. That's what it was all about to my mom: anything that could lead to a baby was considered womanly behavior. Dillan was my first real everything and I fell head over heels over the guy who I knew deep down inside had issues with women. But I had no healthy views on relationships, everything I knew was informed by the trauma in my family. They didn't have the tools either, they were also survivors with no one to give a voice to their pain. I was just happy to feel loved and, more important, protected. Dillan was a lion when it came to me. He would come to my defense in a heartbeat. He always gave me the benefit of the doubt and would ask questions later. One time, a girl started going around telling people that she was going to fight me for no reason. I didn't even know the girl. Then she walked toward me while I was leaving my class one day, and he intercepted her and asked her to move along. To this day I have no idea why that young woman wanted to fight me. I suspect that it had something to do with him. On another occasion, while I was at a party with my friends, a guy groped me and before I could call Dillan, his teammate was already beating the guy up. People knew that messing with me would have its consequences. That made me feel good, it was some sort of weird form of love that I wasn't used to. Looking back at it, I was fed in a way that I longed for as a kid. I had finally found the person that I thought I had been looking for. The man who would show up for me.

Baby Daddy

When my son turned six months old, his father turned on us. Baby Daddy was struggling with school trying to get to the NFL while juggling being a dad and having a girlfriend. He started to pull away. My friends were my family at the time, helping me with everything. I was working at a bank as a teller because I needed money to live. A retail job wasn't enough to take care of us, since I was wearing out my welcome at my friend's place. I had been there for over a year. And I didn't feel like I had a boyfriend anymore. Baby Daddy and I only talked about our kid. We were on and off and it seemed that he didn't really want to be with me anymore. He was seeing other girls, while I was at home lactating and nursing stretch marks. I definitely didn't feel attractive or desirable and I was scared of having sex. My body had gone through so many changes and I had to have an episiotomy. I didn't want anything to go near my lady parts, they had been through enough. I also stopped eating as much because I wanted to lose the weight. I was now competing for my own man with girls who had no babies. I just wanted to see some light at the end of the tunnel. I needed it.

Extreme dieting is how I lost my weight. I wasn't that big but in my head I was. I had been struggling with self-destructive eating habits since I was five years old. I just didn't know what to call it. I was told that I didn't like to eat and was forced to by my family. They just assumed that I didn't want to waste any time because I wanted to be outside playing all the time. I went from 156 pounds to 117 pounds in three months. I ate a boiled egg for breakfast, a scoop of tuna with lettuce for lunch, and a grilled chicken breast with any diuretic vegetable of choice. Oh, and a gallon of water. I lost so much weight that my period stopped.

On my normal Saturday stroll in the mall I met this woman named Marsha Doll. She was a thin, white, Southern woman who spoke fast and sharp. She had on tight white jeans and a low-cut top and had long nails and fancy jewelry. She introduced herself with all the confidence in the world and I liked her. She was a modeling agent and wanted me to come by her office. I thought she was full of shit and that it was probably a scam. I mean, I was standing in the middle of Governor's Square mall pushing a stroller feeling like I weighed eight hundred pounds. This lady had to be kidding. I couldn't be a model. I was a mom. But Marsha meant what she said and didn't give up. She called me and wouldn't stop until I agreed to come talk. I went and saw her and that was the beginning of my modeling career phase two. In truth, I had started when I was in Miami—but had quit because I didn't believe I could do it. Here was Marsha telling me post-child-labor that I had a shot at becoming the next Tyra Banks. I don't know if I really wanted to be a model. I just knew that it was a sexy thing to be, especially for your football player boyfriend. I was so scared of losing him. This could be my way to get him back into me, so I said yes.

But it was already on the way to being over. The stress of taking care of my son and trying to get back to school was too much for the guy who wanted to get drafted. My son had just turned one and I was broke. I needed more money, the one job was not enough. I was really on my own now. No one was going to come save us. The NFL wasn't guaranteed for Dillan and, in any case, that wasn't going to be my money. I had to figure this out. I kept modeling on the side. My friends were pitching in with the baby until I was able to get him into a daycare. I started to move on even though I was crushed. I felt so alone. I lost everything. My family was eight hours away. My friends had their own lives and no kids, Baby Daddy was working on his game on and off the field. It was me and my baby boy. I started to do local runway shows at the department stores and earned enough money to pay rent. I liked the runway, but I wasn't saying anything. It felt like I was getting closer to my calling, but not there yet. Still, I got my own apartment. My life was hectic, but it was looking up. I was a single mom and I was okay with it. My baby was healthy, smart, and safe. Nothing else mattered.

The following summer I went to Georgia with Baby Daddy so that his family could see our child. We were in a vague place in our relationship, which meant he messed around with other people while I was devoted to him. He had just been drafted to the San Francisco 49ers and he was on cloud nine. His family was made up of two sisters and his mom. They were close and very nice—Southern nice. They said ma'am and sir and greeted everyone when they walked into a place. They were more polite than I was used to and very family oriented—they had a big family and were all connected. His mom was a tall, sweet woman with the same eyes as my Baby Daddy. She was soft spoken and treated me well. She helped me as much as she could.

During our visit, I fell into a disagreement with one of his sisters, which led to a major fight between him and me. So much so that Baby Daddy asked me to leave. That solidified the end of our relationship. The disagreement was stupid, but it was enough to get us kicked out of their house.

Richard

I was too embarrassed to call my mom and I still wasn't ready for "I told you so," so I decided to call my uncle Richard, who was living in Virginia at the time. My uncle had a family, he was married with a son and had a life outside of us, but it was worth a try. He and my aunt Hilda paid for me to get on the next flight and took us in without any hesitation. This meant the world to me. My uncle was the one who left. He was my role model and I had so much respect for him. I had been fueled with misinformation from my mother and grandmother about his wife taking him away from the family. They were wrong. He left because he knew that getting away was a shot at a better life.

The visit with my Virginia family was not a long one. They were gracious and generous and loving. I had never seen anyone in my family carry on in this way. It felt peaceful and healthy and they just welcomed me and Baby O right in. Uncle Richard loved my son. He had his own boy and treated mine like he was his too. He took us fishing, we watched movies together, and it was definitely a healing time for me. After the fights with my mom and the failed relationship with Baby Daddy, there wasn't much more for me to mess up. This was what I needed—harmony and family life, something I could experience to later model. I promised myself I would create my own version of this one day. In the meantime, I was enjoying life. I had limited contact with everyone. When Baby Daddy called, I would just hand my son the phone, I had nothing to say. I wasn't ready to talk to my mom yet. I was crafting my plan for life after Virginia. I wanted to go do so many things, and being there made me feel like I actually could. I felt refreshed and inspired. My uncle made a life like that after leaving home at sixteen to join the army. He had a beautiful home that he owned, he and his wife both had nice cars, their son's room was amazing. They vacationed and did things outside of work as a family. They even had a guest room that we fit right into. But above all, they loved each other, had a close family unit, and had a chemistry that was enviable, it was magic. I wanted that.

With enough distance and time, Baby Daddy eventually became curious about me again. I was as aloof as could be, actually getting over him. I started to see my life without him and great things ahead. So naturally he wanted to talk, and when we did from time to time, I just was not into it. The hurt and rejection I had felt when he threw us out of his home—without giving me the benefit of the doubt—broke me. I had always been loyal to him. I turned my back on my family because I believed in us. I shared everything I had with him. And he just threw me away without any hesitation. I didn't have much to say at this point. He was remorseful, and he knew that I wasn't the same girl as before. My voice didn't soften to his manipulation. I was not feeling him and his bullshit anymore. I still loved him but I was so disappointed in him. We were supposed to ride for each other. I didn't care about the NFL or anything associated with it. I was never in it for that. In fact, I resented it. I encouraged him to believe in himself, since I knew he was smart enough to do anything he wanted to. He loved nutrition and wanted to study it further, so I pushed for that. I never reduced him to just being a meal ticket having to be cattle in an industry that didn't care about him as a human being. I always talked to him. I knew that he needed that type of support. He was conditioned to feel that he couldn't do more and I was never going to let the father of my son feel that I saw him that way too. And after all of this, I wasn't sure that I wanted to be with him anymore.

My baby asked for his daddy constantly. They would talk daily. But then the baby would put the phone to my ear to include me. He was going on two now and was talking. He was a funny kid and got joy from seeing others happy. My Baby O's smile was magic. Everywhere we went people would point it out. I wanted everything for him. I wanted a family for him. One that was much like the one I was living with. I began to talk to Baby Daddy more and we started to be friends again. Meanwhile, I was looking for work and checking out places in the DMV area to move to. I was working on my plan. Baby Daddy knew it and started to express that he was afraid he was losing us, but I would never take his son from him. At one point, he had a breakdown and apologized. He was under enormous pressure. He felt like he always had to take care of his family because his father hadn't. I understood exactly where he was coming from and for the first time, we had a heart-to-heart conversation where he was vulnerable. I was right back at that place where he had blasted that 2 Live Crew song in my face. I was still in love with him and there was nothing I could do about it. I started talking to him all the time again. But I kept it a secret. I didn't want my uncle to be mad. He felt that Baby Daddy had not been handling things correctly and didn't believe he had the best intentions. I wasn't telling anyone anything until I felt it was real. A few phone conversations were not going to undo the amount of pain and stress I had been enduring.

After a day of fishing with my uncle, cousin, and son, I got back to the house and flowers were sitting at the doorstep. They were from Baby Daddy and they were beautiful. Lilies, my favorite. When they were delivered, my aunt knew they were for me and thought it would be a sweet surprise for me to see them as soon as I got to the house. A letter had come in the mail addressed to me that day too. I had no idea who it was from, but when I opened it, the handwriting looked familiar. It was written on San Francisco 49ers letterhead. Baby Daddy wrote about what had happened and apologized, spoke to my concerns, and ended with a marriage proposal that I could present to my uncle. I was supposed to say yes. This would repair the relationship with my mom and family. I would no longer be a baby momma. I would be a wife. My son would have what I had always wanted him to have and I would live far away from my family, just like my uncle.

But something deep down inside didn't feel right to me. It was as if right when I was at the cusp of getting my life and independence, something would show up to take it away. I just had to believe in myself to give it a try. Baby Daddy would be there if it was meant to be. It was not time for me to get married, and a baby was not the reason to say yes. Still, I knew that this was the only thing that could fix things in my mother's eyes, and I valued what she thought way more than what I thought. That night I tossed and turned and asked my aunt to tell him I was sleeping when he called. I was unsure about what I wanted to do and had a hard time putting myself first, that felt like I was being selfish.

The next morning when my aunt came into the room to hand me the phone, I had decided that I was going to tell him that I wasn't ready for marriage. But when I said hello, it was my grandmother. I hadn't spoken to her in a while and was so happy to hear her voice. I told her what had happened. She just listened and gave me no advice. She was calling to hear my voice and tell me that she loved us. And just as we were going to hang up, the other line rang. It was Baby Daddy. I couldn't avoid him anymore. He asked me what was going on and I could hear his heaviness. I gave him the yes he wanted, even though I felt that it was a mistake. I did it for my baby, my mom, my grandmother, him, and everyone else who needed it. That was the way I was built. I didn't know how to do it any other way yet. I thought maybe this would lead me to the family unit and magic my uncle Richard had created, a life I deeply wanted to call my own one day.

We celebrated that night. Baby Daddy had his yes and I had my lilies.

El Sapo y La Vaca

It was very common to see in-laws not like each other on television, many times it was framed as comical. In *All in the Family* it was Archie who hated his son-in-law Michael (who he called "Meathead") for their differences in viewpoints on social issues. My grandmother and my stepfather were no exception in real life, they could not stand each other. My grandmother referred to my stepfather as "El Sapo," which means frog, and he would call her "La Vaca," cow. He also would refer to her as "Ordinaria" and would often describe her as ugly. One of their biggest issues was cultural. My stepfather being a white Cuban man saw my grandmother as less than because she had more Black features, hence the nickname, which referred to having Afrocentric features. He would remind her often of her Black blood, which she was very proud of by the way. They made it a Puerto Rican versus Cuban thing, but in reality it was just a white supremacy, anti-Blackness thing. The battle of who was better was an ongoing one, a lot of back-and-forth. Sometimes it was actually funny, but it was always rooted in ignorance. These events would escalate and at times they'd get very ugly. It was known that these two did not like each other, and should never have to interact, unless it was completely necessary, so we tried our best to keep them apart.

On one of those days when I was a preteen, dealing with raging hormones, along with all the other bullshit that was my living situation, my stepfather and I had an exchange. I can't quite remember what it was about, but it was often something as trivial as me getting in trouble because I would not entertain my younger brother to help him eat. I had to jump around and dance and be a jester so that they could trick him into eating. I usually complied because I didn't want to see my little brother getting hit, but sometimes I was just tired and didn't want to do it and that would land me in the doghouse. Other times it was because I didn't wake up early enough to brush my teeth and wash my face on a Saturday, because that is what you're supposed to do on the weekend. Or it could just be that I was having one of those days where I could no longer handle the bullshit and I'd talk back. Whatever our exchanges were about, I just knew that he didn't like me and felt that I was in the way, so any moment that he had to scold me was an opportunity for him to exercise the hate that he had in his heart for me. On that particular day, I tested his limits, and he felt justified in hitting me. But I wasn't prepared to take it. There was an unfamiliar rage boiling within me and before I knew it, I rushed to the kitchen, grabbed a cutting knife, and took it straight to his neck. Honestly, I don't know where I got that from because I was no gangster. I think I might've seen it on television. Instead of him being concerned, or disturbed by it, I felt as if he found it amusing and almost exciting. I guess he realized that gave him an opportunity to do something even worse because now he was really in the right. But before he could fully react and do any real damage, I managed to get to the phone to call my grandmother, and she immediately came to my rescue. Now, my grandmother always carried her gun, her .38 Special, and the last thing I wanted was for this to escalate in violence and land her in jail. We were often driven by guilt for telling on the people who would do bad things to us who belonged to our family, and labeled a troublemaker if a man went to jail because of something we said or did. We were shamed into protecting the predators who lurked around us, and that kept many of us quiet. But I felt like I was in real danger, and I had had enough. That day, I was willing to deal with the consequences of telling on this man.

My abuela walked in swinging, she immediately attacked him. She didn't ask any questions, she was there to rescue me. My mother jumped in the middle, but my stepfather pushed her away. At five foot seven, my grandmother was a fairly tall woman and pretty strong. But she was not strong enough to fight off that man, and every ounce of hate that was consuming him at the time. And that day I saw this man hit my hero, he was reckless and abusive. He exploited the fact that we lived by a code. He knew that my mom would never tell because my uncles would beat his ass and that would cause them to go to jail. She also didn't want her man to catch it, she was in love with him. He also knew that she would manipulate me into not saying anything as well. So he took his liberties and put his hands on my grandmother, and as much as she fought back, she could not take him down. It was a sad day for me, I hadn't wanted any harm to come to my grandmother, I just didn't know what to do or who to call. I felt responsible for what happened, and I was told as much. I believe it was me who talked her out of shooting my stepfather because it would ruin her life and mine.

What I learned that day was that, for the most part, men were stronger than women, and we needed a man to protect us from the bad men. After that terrible incident, I started to feel that not having a man in my life was a deficit, there was no one to protect me. And it became a priority.

I Chose Violence

Though I wouldn't do my first show until 2008, I initially moved to Los Angeles in 2000 with my two children to pursue a career as an actor and a writer. I wrote my first script to star in and it had made it to the next round of a big screenwriter's competition. I decided to make movies. I was always looking for signs in life—still talking to trees, reading the stars, searching for anything that would give me hope. Even though I was a soon-to-be divorced single mom, I was still young. Many successful women in Hollywood older than thirty-five were killing it and I was in my twenties. I believed I had a shot. I had been living in Miami for almost two years with my kids while my husband figured his life out. He was in and out, bouncing between my place and his football buddies' homes in other states.

I was speaking often about my desires and told my closest friends what I wanted to do with my life. I dared to dream. I had put my goals and dreams on hold to support my family, my mother, Baby Daddy, and my children. It was time to go after what I wanted while

I was young enough to do it. I knew that moving to California would be the move; no one wanted to come here. It would be my place. I could start a new life like my uncle Richard did.

My marriage took a turn for the worse and it was time for me to get out of there. We were fighting all the time and the children were starting to see it. The more I sought my independence, the more hostile things became. We loved each other but there was just so much pain between us. He couldn't let the NFL lifestyle go and I didn't fit in. I just wanted to be my own person and live out my dreams. I was never really a part of that world. I didn't fit in with the wives, many of them were elitist, materialistic bitches. I was a kid and honestly didn't get what they were about. Lunch and shopping dates didn't fulfill me, I wanted to be my own star. My identity was important to me. I once went to a player's wife's outing and refused to identify as my husband's wife, I instead said that he was my husband. It was met with scoff and judgment. They were not my vibe, except for a woman whom I considered my one real friend on the team, Diann. She actually took care of me when my daughter was born because the guys were off at training camp. The NFL was the worst thing that ever happened to us, it was a wicked world rooted in corruption and systemic oppression and it hurt more families than it helped. I decided that I was going to go figure out my life, alone. I had enough at this point.

I was an intern at Luke Records at the time and worked for Luther "Uncle Luke" Campbell, former leader of 2 Live Crew. This was a full circle moment for me! That man trusted me in ways I didn't even trust myself at the time. He is a great part of the reason I decided to leave to conquer the life I wanted. This is where I learned how to demand and manage my money, as well as to engage in local politics and to understand that government was for me too. While the world saw a man who was throwing parties and exploiting women, I was being mentored by a businessman who empowered minorities and challenged the powers that be. He taught me so much, I am ever so grateful to him, he is one of the reasons I was strong enough to leave and brave enough to use my voice. I had come to develop an entirely different point of view about this man.

Luke had one of the most efficient assistants I had ever encountered; she was on it. I learned how to book travel and to pay attention to detail through her. I use that now in my own life and career as a touring comedian. One of my duties was to make sure that Luke's travel was booked and done so correctly, so I communicated heavily with his preferred travel agent. She and I became friends. We discussed our lives along with everything else. She was originally from the Midwest and had moved to Central Florida with her family. I went back to Miami after leaving San Diego with my two kids. We shared a lot with each other. She was older and wiser and would often give me advice. She also had her own business and that was inspiring to me. I wanted to be financially independent. She was gracious and kind enough to get me three tickets to LA on loan. That was a vote of confidence. She was recently divorced with three children and had started her own business that was flourishing and now she was encouraging me to go start a new life. We were both at a new place in our lives and she became a big supporter of mine.

Even though I had lived on the West Coast previously with my husband, the difference between living in San Diego and Los Angeles was the difference between security and freedom. While living in San Diego as a married woman to an NFL player meant not having to worry about my finances, living on my own in LA allowed me the space to make my own decisions, have agency over my person, and dare to do the things that I wanted so badly. It was time for me to grow up and go get my life.

I had one friend in LA—LaWanda. I had met her through another friend and we stayed in touch. She extended the invite for me to come to LA, and offered her home as the landing place for us until I was able to find my footing. I moved into an apartment that she had once shared with her mother. It was a condo that they'd been renting for a long time in Culver City, Los Angeles. It was a quiet, suburban area where we saw families, which meant it was kid friendly. The two-bedroom apartment was beautiful. I shared one room with my kids. I believe she had some sort of subsidy program with the state, which allowed her to have very low rent. That enabled her to allow me time there for very little money, and in this way, I was able to save. It was a mixed apartment complex, some units bought, some rented, and housed a combination of all types of families, singles, working-class people, and a lot of children. It also had a pool, tennis courts, and a security gate, which meant there were no surprise visits, something that was essential to me. I always feared that Baby Daddy would pop up whenever he felt like it. My kids needed stability after the NFL and I could also use some peace. During the time we were together, we moved around a lot: Miami, Tallahassee, Georgia, Virginia, San Diego. After that, I went back to Miami and now my eight-year-old son, four-year-old daughter, and me were in Los Angeles. We were settling down, no more moving.

Since I was taking care of the children on my own, I immediately set out to look for work. My personal focus was to heal from my marriage and everything else. I had work to do. This was another chance at life. I knew that I had to evolve and get past the issues, otherwise, the move would be pointless. I would just be transferring my traumas to a new place. I kept hearing the term "doing the work" but didn't really understand what it meant. I met a friend named Kim, who was in therapy, she explained it to me. Therapy? I had never had a friend that I ever knew to be in therapy. That was such a foreign concept for me. My whole life I was told that the people that go to therapy are crazy. I wasn't crazy, but I could really use some help sorting out my life.

The more people I met in California, the more I heard about others going to therapy. I read one self-help book after the other. I started with *Yesterday, I Cried*, followed by *Awaken the Giant Within*, and then I found another and another and kept going. Readers are leaders, Mrs. Flannagan was always in the back of my head. I experienced a spiritual cleansing, learning how to unpack my trauma, but I still had a long way to go. That was a long year for me. I was still in shock that my marriage and family as I knew it failed. I blamed myself. There was no dad in our home anymore, that was my fault for leaving. But I wasn't planning on remarrying. I didn't want my kids to experience a stepfather, so I made that vow to myself. As unhealthy as that may have been, it felt good. My kids were going to be safe.

I was getting lost all over the place, trying to make friends and adapting to this new climate. Miami was hot all the time, but Los Angeles got cold at night. I did not like being cold. I attempted to make friends in the complex with the parents of some of the children that my kids played with. They were either older or married and didn't like having a younger woman around their husbands. One of my neighbors actually said to me, "I like you but my husband has those roaming eyeballs and I don't want any problems." That was weird. Another woman my age whom I met through a co-worker uninvited me from brunch at her place when she found out I was bringing my children. She said that she couldn't be friends with me because I had kids and she couldn't relate; we were in two different places in our lives. I thought I was never going to make friends.

Wednesday was a short day for my daughter at school, so it became my laundry day because that meant I could wash clothes before it got dark. I didn't like to go to the laundry room at night. There were barely lights on in the complex and it felt creepy when it was empty. I still battled with many childhood fears, the dark was one of them. I still slept with the lights on. I don't know what I was afraid of, but it was real.

I developed my routine and things were starting to flow. I volunteered at my daughter's school one day out of the week and at my son's on another. I was consulting as a promotional rep for music labels, so I was able to work from home. I cooked and cleaned on the weekends. And Wednesdays I would take the kids to play outside with the other kids, while I washed clothes. This may sound routine to someone else but to me it was new. I had been living my life on other people's whims since I was born.

As I loaded my whites one day, this tall, brown man walked in, talking on his phone while he switched his clothes from the washer to the dryer. He was fine. I stared at him as he threw those dryer sheets in his load all while holding the phone between his shoulder and his ear. I realized where I knew him from. He was the guy from a singing group I really liked. He was taller than I thought, and had an amazing body. His scent was so strong, I could smell him from the other side of the room—Armani's Gio, I knew that cologne. Mixed with his own body chemistry, it was something else. It was familiar. But I continued to tend to my own laundry, minding my own business, trying not to stare. I picked up my bleach from the ground to pour into my machine, turned around, and awkwardly met his eyes—he had been waiting for me to look. We smiled at each other, it felt good to be seen. I didn't really know how to flirt but I gave it my best attempt. He talked on the phone but continued to look and smile at me. I just stood there and blushed, I couldn't believe it, someone was looking at me. I felt so unattractive and undesirable, being told repeatedly that no man was going to want a divorced woman with two kids. Someone went as far as to tell me that having Black kids would make it even harder. I was ready to be alone forever because no one was going to mistreat me or my beautiful kids.

My four-year-old daughter stormed in like the Tasmanian devil and crashed right into my legs, and the Clorox spilled everywhere. It was as if she knew that something was about to go down and it was not happening on her watch. He and I both laughed. Then he introduced himself anyway—she didn't scare him off. I blushed the entire time, "I'm Aida, nice to meet you." My baby girl held onto my right leg the entire time until he left.

His name was John and he had been in LA only two years. The second time we saw each other, we crossed paths at the mailbox and talked for a while. I shared with him that I didn't know many people in the city and had recently relocated from Miami, and he insisted that I take his number and call him if I needed anything. He was from Chicago and was still getting used to the people and culture of Southern California. Moving from Chicago to Southern California is like microwaving a Hot Pocket, steaming hot but still cold on the inside. The first time we talked, it was for hours. My kids were at school and I sat on a chair in my living room and had a four-hour conversation with a person who was just one building away from me. We had a lot of things in common. We both read satire and fantasy and loved *Star Wars*. We were both into the supernatural, we believed that aliens were among us. We grew up in church and both referenced scripture. I felt a connection, but our relationship was platonic. He was in a relationship. I was casually dating. I wasn't looking for anything serious.

We kept talking and sharing our lives with each other, as friends. I learned a lot from him about the male perspective. I had a skewed view of men and how they operated. He helped me with that, he gave me dating advice. We never saw each other, we just talked on the phone. I was busy being a mom and he was working as a musician, but we always stayed in touch. He was my first real friend in Los Angeles after LaWanda.

Over the course of a year, I heard so many stories about what was happening in his relationship I became his confidant. We really gave each other therapy, we each had someone who would listen. We laughed at our situations often and we had a safe place to unload. Our friendship flourished that year. We talked every day.

John had a good head on his shoulders. He gave me career advice and always encouraged me to stay in the Word. He was also raised in the church. He would go on about Hollywood and its disconnect from God. He was raised by believing parents and his father stayed on him—he loved his dad, he talked to him every day.

And then one day, he asked me to lunch and something changed. I sat and talked with him about everything for hours. We laughed and flirted like we had never done before. I felt like a woman for the first time in a long while. We had such a good time at lunch, we went out on a date that night and a spark was ignited. I guess the undeniable attraction that had been there from the very beginning reached the surface. We were honest about it and decided to start dating. He and his girlfriend had broken up and she had moved away.

The relationship with him was its own thing. We spent lots of time talking and did a lot together. We ate all over the place and worked out at the gym together. He rode a motorcycle and took me on my first ride. It was all quite romantic. Meanwhile, I got a more stable job working at a private bank and making more money, so I was able to move into my own place in the San Fernando Valley. This meant a better school district for my kids. Me leaving the complex made our relationship better. We had some space. I was in Sherman Oaks, which is about twenty minutes away, depending on traffic. I was separated and working on my divorce, honestly still trying to figure myself out, learning how to date, which I never did, and learning what I wanted. But I was also enjoying being with someone and still feeling free.

Getting into this relationship was fun and, at first, we did so much together. It still felt fresh once we were several months in. We went dancing and grabbed pancakes. He was thoughtful of my schedule and planned events during the day while the kids were in school. The chemistry was through the roof, we were falling in love. We had a lot of fun together. Even when we weren't doing anything, we were in this space that was magical because we could just sit and talk and connect, not having to go anywhere. We would cook together. I made my arroz con gandules and he made his salmon. We would eat and watch television. *Friday After Next* was one of our faves. We rewound Katt Williams's scenes over and over and just laughed. We went to the movie theater early in the mornings, after dropping my kids off at school, to see *The Lord of the Rings* or *The Matrix* trilogy. All the things that I enjoyed, he enjoyed, I had found my partner in crime.

Like most relationships, it was great at the beginning, while we were in our honeymoon stage. We saw each other all the time, more than when we lived within feet of each other. I was enjoying it and just wanted to be in his presence always. He made me feel good. It was euphoric. I got butterflies in my stomach when I saw him. He awakened all parts of me.

The beautiful part about it was that he knew I had children from the start and was very respectful of that and had a high level of consideration for my kids. He would include them in our outings, suggesting that we do things with them. That was very refreshing coming from someone who was young, hot, and in demand. He was popular women would throw themselves at him left and right. And he was taking my kids and me to see *Shrek* and then to Chuck E. Cheese. You could see that he came from a good family by the way he treated mine. He had a Baptist Black upbringing in Chicago and was very connected to home. His perception of fatherhood was very different from mine because he grew up with his dad and had a special relationship with him. His father was his everything: his confidant, his best friend, his spiritual advisor. He adored his dad and he only hoped to be one someday, too, so he could show up like his own father did. I was enamored by all of this.

Because of my past traumas with my mom's boyfriends, and those who became my stepfathers, it took me a year and a half to allow him around my kids. I wanted to be very careful about who I brought around. He eventually became like a father to my kids, doing homework with them and disciplining them in a very thoughtful way. Rather than raise his voice, he'd talk to them when they did things that required redirection, employing positive reinforcement. We became a unit and we did many things together, like going to the movies, to Universal Studios, to Magic Mountain. I wasn't alone anymore. I had someone that was present for it all.

It was very refreshing to have someone to share those moments with, not just for fun, but to help carry the load. I was living in a city by myself where I didn't have my mom or my brothers and sister. I didn't have any help and I really didn't have a lot of friends. He was like my best friend and he was around. He would go to the kids' talent shows with me and sometimes even for me. One time, I had to work and I wasn't able to make one of my daughter's shows, and he showed up for her, watched the show, and then took her and her best friend to dinner afterward. That for me was quite admirable. He didn't have any children, so he didn't know how to be a dad from personal experience, but because of what he had lived with his own father, he had some ideas and was able to share that with my kids.

John never judged me, he accepted me as I was. It was always "Be free to be who you really want to be. Don't be afraid. Show up. Show out." And that was what I needed at the time. I was embracing my womanhood, tapping into my sexy side. Appreciating my beauty and walking in it. He brought that out of me, he always told me that I was a force and I believed him. He always made me feel seen. It was going great. We were in our own little world.

On Thanksgiving of 2004, I was preparing to go on a trip to Yosemite with my children and friends. We were going to celebrate the holiday there. It would be the first time I ever went to a cabin and had an outdoor nontraditional holiday without my extended family. For me, Thanksgiving also had its trauma from my childhood, so I was working on reframing that by creating new positive memories with my loved ones. At home in Miami we would have a traditional meal, sitting around the table having generic conversations, and arguments and accusations would fly around. But ultimately, we would have a good time because we were together, listening to Latin music and eating pigeon peas and rice. Going to a cabin was something quite different, but I was excited about doing it with my kids because it was something new and we declared it part of our new adventure in California. My kids were so excited to be going to this park—my son had read all about it and my daughter loved the outdoors.

As I packed for our trip, my home phone rang. I didn't even think when I reached and grabbed the phone. The woman on the other end was not a familiar voice. She called me by my name, "Aida, you know who this is?"

"I don't," I replied. "Can you tell me who it is because I have to go."

"This is Alexis."

"Okay, I don't know who Alexis is," I replied.

"Think hard. This is Alexis, John's girlfriend."

I took a beat. I had no idea what she was talking about, so I let her continue talking. She wanted to know why we had been talking so much—she had checked his phone. This was the girl that he had been dating before me, the one who moved. Apparently, they were still in a relationship despite him telling me that the relationship had been over for more than a year.

In that moment, I crumbled. My friends, who stopped by to pick us up, had to catch me. One of my closest friends, Kibi, was the one who pretty much scraped me up off the ground, put me back together again, and said, "Let's go, we're going to go to the mountains. The phones won't work and you'll have an opportunity to just breathe, unpack, decompress, and also enjoy your holiday with your children, which you deserve and so do they."

Kibi has always been a force in my life, from the moment we met not long after I moved to the Valley. I met her in a parking lot of a nightclub that I went to after finally finding a sitter who I felt I could trust. It was love at first sight with her—the minute I met her I knew I wanted us to be friends. She was a fearless, confident, and powerful Harvard grad who had a lot of fire and is one of the most intelligent people I have ever met. Although she was younger than me and our upbringings were widely different, we still had many things in common. Not having our dads was one of them. But in her eyes, it was his loss. Seeing that was key for me. I needed that perspective in my life. She was successful without her father in her life, I needed that same energy. Going to a cabin in the woods for Thanksgiving was something I would only do with her—she was big on doing things that were adventurous and commonly framed as "white people shit."

And so we left. We went to Yosemite. It was bittersweet, a beautiful weekend where my children got to explore and experience things they had never seen before. Hiking at Yosemite and a cabin, we saw deer and wildlife freely running around. They went ice-skating for the first time. It was a great holiday weekend, even if I was dying on the inside and filled with pain and rage. I was so mad at myself for opening myself up and trusting someone, allowing them in, and being betrayed. And still I was in this beautiful place watching my kids experience nature and have so much fun. It was a constant tug-of-war within me. I made the best of it and did everything I could to protect my kids from what was my horrible reality at the time. I just focused on my kids and got my joy from there. It was so cool to see them doing things that they had only seen on television, like rock climbing and fishing. I actually wished our trip lasted longer than a long weekend. I dreaded going back to face my situation with my lying boyfriend and his girlfriend.

That was one long drive back for me. Anxiety gripped my chest. I kept wondering when I was going to hear from him. If I was going to at all. I was so upset and at the same time needed to know where I stood with him. I did this thing in my head where I needed to know what I meant to him. I don't know why that's what I cared about at the time. He had cheated and lied to us, I felt like a fool, and still I wanted him to choose me, like he was some prize. I knew what he had done and still wanted him to love me. I needed to hear his explanation as if whatever he was going to say would justify the hurt that he caused me. That Monday, when we finally drove into my neighborhood and approached my place, I quickly noticed his car was parked out front. I felt relieved. He cared enough about me to show up. Maybe there was hope for us after all. As soon as we arrived at the complex where I was living, John was waiting for us at the door. He looked tired and sad. He was also embarrassed. He followed us into my place, my kids went upstairs to wash up. They knew something was up since they didn't even try to hang out like they normally would. John immediately grabbed me for a hug and began to apologize profusely. He insisted that it was a misunderstanding. He told me that the woman was lying and that he had been negligent in not drawing the line with her. He had maintained a friendship with her after their breakup but she insisted on them continuing their relationship. He assured me that their relationship was over and that he had put it all to a stop. He then rushed upstairs and apologized to my children for hurting their mother. My kids had no idea what was going on but they knew something was wrong. I believed him because I wanted to believe in the best of him. I didn't want to believe that he would play games with my babies, not him. He was a family man. So, we continued our relationship.

He was involved in my life and in so many things that I did. He was a part of my friend group. Relatives knew who he was. My sister came out for a while to stay with me and she met him and we did things together. My best friends all knew him and we would go out and hang. So we went on with life, and put the past in the past. That's what I told myself to get through. I knew that something was off and though I didn't wholeheartedly believe the woman who called me, I knew that she wasn't completely lying either. I didn't really trust him anymore. I questioned everything he did. I decided that he would not sleep over at my place, and he never objected. I didn't feel comfortable with him being home with my kids. We were definitely not having that *Jerry Maguire* moment when the kid wakes up to a shirtless man eating his cereal. The feeling of waking up at home with a man who wasn't their father didn't sit well with me. It was a very uncomfortable feeling that I experienced as a child and I never wanted my own kids to feel that. If there were going to be any sleepovers, it would only be their friends.

We were together for three more years. Even though I felt it wasn't right, I wasn't willing to let go. I had to make this work. I needed my family and friends to see that this was real. I thought that this relationship validated me. I wasn't some single mom that he was sleeping with. I was his woman. There were instances where he would show up in a way that was so endearing and sweet. That always reminded me that I was in something special with someone that I was in love with. He was willing to do anything that I would ask, like dancing salsa, which he didn't know how to do but was willing to learn. He would have Spanish food and eat what he wasn't used to. We went on trips that included the kids, he encouraged and held them up in everything. From school to God to sports, he was there for it all.

I continued the journey with him because it was comfortable, but I also cannot deny that I was completely in love with the man. I was in a good place or at least I wanted to believe that I was. I kept trying to convince myself that we had such a good thing because he afforded me the space. He also showed up for me. He encouraged me and the woman that I was becoming. I was growing up and making decisions on my own, without consulting with my family back home. He was the best friend that I thought I needed in this new space of mine as I was growing up and raising children, and becoming a version of myself that I never thought I could be: independent and believing that I could do it on my own. That was very important to me because it was something that I never thought I could do. In many ways, he also stimulated and showed up for me artistically. As a writer and an actor, I was excited about the possibility of where this could go because this was a version of a relationship that I had only imagined. Someone who would support my creative dreams was ideal compared to what I had been involved in before, where I felt restricted, suppressed, and controlled. So we continued to move along even if I always felt that I couldn't trust him as far as I could see him.

The red flags kept showing up and I kept ignoring them. He kept his phone on silent, would always place it face down so that I couldn't see the caller ID. He would disappear at night after leaving my place and tell me that he fell asleep the next day. I was willing to overlook so much just to be with him. It was real and mine, and at least I had someone. I had no idea of what a healthy relationship was. I didn't really understand what it looked like, so I was willing to accept things that might be harmful to me because I didn't know any better. I was enamored with the situation and what I thought it could be, romanticizing an ideal relationship. What I did with my notion of a father I was now doing with a romantic partner.

In total we were together on and off for about five or six years. A lot of times, I didn't really understand how things were affecting me and how they moved me in a way that was not conducive to my progress and mental health. I just stayed because I was afraid to move on. I didn't believe that anyone else would want me, I didn't know I was worthy of a good love.

There was a lot of breaking up and getting back together. From

2001 to 2006, I was in and out of this thing with him. The discoveries of his lies kept coming. I found out about different women and different relationships that he was having. He was just deceiving all the women involved, making us all feel like we were in the same type of relationship with him. We were all in this alleged monogamous relationship with him that was exclusive, and there was a time when there were four of us. I, unfortunately, was the only one with children and my kids were also involved in this relationship with this man. They were attached and cared about him; he was a father figure in their lives.

Even though I knew he was a liar and a cheater, I think my self-esteem at that time was so low, I thought that that was the best I could do. I kept going back to what I had been consistently told in the past: there was no future for me with a good man. Here I was dating this guy who was a working musician, attractive, successful, and desired by many, and he was with me. For some reason I did not believe that I could go out and meet someone else that would be better for me. I didn't want to accept the truth that these women were also victims because he would villainize them and frame it as if they were the ones who wanted him. I made him the prize.

It was really a tough time and as much as I talked about wanting to be far away from my relatives and my friends, I missed my village, my grandmother, and my uncles. They weren't perfect but they were there for me. It took me moving away to realize just how much my family really meant to me. I let myself focus so much on my failed marriage that I didn't allow myself to see how my tribe did the best they could. The friends I had in California were new friends. Honestly, I was embarrassed and ashamed to share with them what was happening to me because I had been putting on this whole performance of being in this ideal relationship for a long time now. It was a rough spot to be in, but I remained there because, at the time, it was really all I thought I had.

After every single situation that pointed to lies and deceit, I would find a reason to ignore it and sweep it under the rug. I was not ready to let go. I didn't know *how* to let go. No one had ever taught me how to handle this kind of situation. What I had experienced in my life was women holding on to a man until they secured another, for fear of not being alone. For me, it was a behavior that I would have to unlearn if I truly wanted to have a life of success, peace, and happiness. I continued to date John nonexclusively. He was the one person I felt safe having sex with, I wasn't ready to move on. Every phase of our relationship became more about what he wanted and less about me. I negotiated my soul's deepest desires away for temporary moments that eventually became unfulfilling.

The night before Mother's Day in 2006, after a long meeting, I went out with a co-worker. I had my sitter that night and could actually have some me time. We went to a place called The White Lotus in Hollywood. It was the current hot spot, a full sushi restaurant on one side and nightclub on the other.

John promised to join us, but he took forever. He was out doing his usual dirt. At this point, I already knew that this is how he operated, thanks to my new therapist I was planning an exit strategy. I was having a good time with my co-worker Lewis, dancing our life away to whatever new Beyoncé song was out. It was all good until the strippers showed up. I had no problems with dancers, I had worked with them when I worked at Luke Records. But this particular group of women came to the club to start shit. These women decided to surround me at the club and what I thought was a girl power moment was actually bullying. One of the girls kept flinging her hair in my face, she would move every time I moved. It became apparent that she was fucking with me. She was the one who told me that they were dancers at a local club and that I needed to move. "They want to see us dance, that's what we do! Step back with your wannabe Barbie ass." After multiple times of me asking them to please stop, one of them decided to mush me in my forehead and I decided to punch her in the face. They probably thought being outnumbered would fill me with fear. I was too angry to count that day. I was hurt, humiliated, and furious at life. I had nothing but rage to offer the young dancer from the Spearmint Rhino, as she taunted me right before my right fist dusted her jaw.

My friend separated us, he grabbed me and moved me away while trying to contain his laughter. We finally went about our business. Yet I suddenly realized how much anger I was carrying, and this relationship was heavily driving that. I knew it was bad. I mean, I actually picked up this young woman and almost threw her over a rail. If I would've been successful in that, I would probably still be in jail. Imagine getting arrested for fighting in a club with a stripper on the night before Mother's Day because I was mad at some dude. That was unacceptable.

John finally made it to the club and when he saw that my hair was disheveled and that I looked out of sorts, he assumed that I had sex with someone else in the club, because of course, if that's what you do, that's what you think other people do. He thought that I was lying about being in an altercation with another woman and that I had probably been in a bathroom getting it on with another man. How specific. I exploded on him. He was a cheater and now was projecting that shit onto me. We had to leave, since our interaction was far more volatile than my previous fight.

We got in his car. As he was driving me to mine, he began to flirt with another woman who pulled up to his window. That was his way of getting back at me, he said, but that's just who he really was. He carried on in my face as if I wasn't there. The level of anger, pain, rage, frustration that fueled me forced me to turn around and hit him as hard as I could. I punched him in the face too. I was two for two. Only I wasn't. John pressed down on the gas and as he sped up, he reached over my lap, opened the passenger door, and pushed me out. I rolled on the ground, covering my face to protect myself. When I finally stopped, I picked myself up and charged toward my vehicle. I had passed the anger and gone straight into sadness. I kept thinking, *How could I allow myself to be in this type of situation? Why did I ignore my feelings for so long?* I felt embarrassed and ashamed and guilty for even allowing myself to still be in this relationship and allowing my children to be a part of it as well.

As I reached my car, I heard him call my name and realized he was close and no longer in his truck. At this point, I was afraid of him because I knew what he was capable of doing. This wasn't the first time he had exhibited this behavior. We had a prior incident where I stayed away from him for a day following my therapist's advice. It was a twenty-four-hour fast so that I could think and clear my head. He stalked me outside of my apartment, parked on the other side, and waited for me to get home to see who I was with. When I pulled up in my car and he saw that I was by myself, he accused me of cheating and yelled at me through the window of my car. I tried to ignore him and attempted to pull away, but he reached in through my window, put my car in park, opened the door, and dragged me out of the car. He emptied a water bottle on me, yelling that the only reason he wouldn't hurt me was because of my children. That had already happened and I was still with him. I had swept that under the rug along with all the other things. And here we were, in this moment, where he was calling my name after tossing me out of a moving vehicle like I was a piece of trash. He had already threatened me before and I was tired of his shit. I don't make excuses for my behavior, I was wrong for hitting him, I should have just left. But I wasn't evolved, I wasn't mature, I was surviving in life. I had just had enough of the disrespect and lies and mistreatment and I honestly didn't know how to deal. I began to pick up the pace toward my car. As the valet approached my vehicle, he charged toward me. I only remember holding on to my car door, kicking him, digging my heel into his chest, and pushing him away from me. I then jumped in my car and sped off. I remember calling one of my friends at the time and telling her the story. I was crying and screaming, in enormous physical and emotional pain, and she thought it was funny. Someone I thought to be one of my closest friends found this scene humorous. I had been on a roller coaster with this guy for so long that people around me didn't take it seriously anymore. I was the boy who cried wolf.

When I got home, two police officers were waiting for me at my door. He had called them and accused me of attacking him. He was trying to protect himself because he knew what he did and that was cause for legal action. He made me out to be the attacker but when the woman cop saw me, she immediately assumed I was the victim. This was a six-foot-four man who weighed more than two hundred pounds, whose hands were registered with the police department as weapons because he was a ten-plus black belt. She asked me if I needed medical attention and they walked me to my door.

That was the end for me. That type of anger and violence reminded me of my own childhood. It could be inflicted upon my children. And that is what eventually ran me away. At that moment, I loved my kids more than I loved myself. And there was no way I would ever let anyone put hands on them. I now felt like it was impossible with him, I no longer trusted him.

The next day when I sat down with my kids for our traditional Mother's Day brunch—we'd go to a different place every year and eat a buffet; we loved the omelet station and getting the crab legs—my son noticed my limp. He then asked me why I had scuff marks on my knees and elbows, and I told him that Mommy had fallen. I was so disgusted with myself because I knew that those were the things women who were abused said to their children to cover up for the men who hurt them. But fuck it, I wasn't sharing that with them, they were too good for it. I ate my crab legs and thought to myself, *It's over. And I won that fight.*

Señorita Gone Wild

The night I decided to have sex for the first time I made the decision at a fraternity party in Tallahassee while ordering a drink—a Malibu and pineapple punch. I wasn't supposed to be there. I was a minor, and I could have caused the program that I was in big problems. But I was away from home, in a reckless mood, feeling I was in charge of myself, and I wanted to do some wild stuff. I was growing up and I was changing. I had spent my entire life being told to be a good girl and to me that meant not being myself. It meant being performative and fake and pretending to be something I was not. I was a good human being and I always tried to do the right thing, but this idea that I could do no wrong was heavy and unrealistic. At the end of the day, I was just a person like everyone else. What I also found disingenuous was being told to do everything right by people who were always doing everything wrong. I just wanted to live my life and have my experiences without unrealistic expectations hanging over my head.

I was making out with my boyfriend for months and having these feelings that I couldn't explain. I wanted more but felt shame at the same time. I would stop myself from being touched because I wanted to keep my virginity intact. That hymen was where my value was, or at least that was what I was constantly being told by my mom and grandmother. It was actually the one attribute that they most pointed out about me. It came before any of my other accomplishments. The honor roll, debating the future second lady Tipper Gore, starting my own nonprofit—none of it mattered more than me being a virtuous young lady.

But at the party, I made my decision, even if only in my mind. I was ready to give up the entire title of "La Señorita." That was how my family referred to me. I just wanted to enjoy life and be a regular girl. I wanted to go out, have fun, party, and experiment. Sex was something that I really wanted to do. I had mixed feelings about it since I knew what it was. And honestly, being molested as a kid had awakened the conflict of wanting to do something that was natural and feeling terrible about it at the same time. Dillan didn't put that much pressure on me, though. He thought it would happen when it was supposed to. Plus, I am sure he was having sex with other girls. He definitely compartmentalized us: I was his girlfriend and future wife; the others were groupies and side chicks. There were levels in that too. Some were just for sex, others were for conversation, and some were hybrids. I listened in on many of the conversations he had with his teammates and friends. I knew what was going on, but I pretended that I didn't. I was proud to be on his arm as the precious girlfriend. Everyone else was just a dumb bitch he was playing with. That night after the party I had another drink and I believe that what I was feeling was horniness. I couldn't even say that word at the time. I just wanted to feel the person that I loved on a different level. I also believed that if he had me, he would want for no one else. It was a sure win in my head, I was conscious of all the attention he would get for being an athlete and I had the power to shut it all down with my untouched, prized vagina.

When I arrived at Dillan's room he was playing video games with his friend. They played *Madden*, it was always *Madden*. I strolled in like I was on a fashion runway. I was feeling myself that night. I wore some brown jeans with an olive-green, off-the-shoulder top and my hair was slicked back. I didn't wear much makeup, just my signature black eyeliner and fuchsia pink lips. But when I saw him my heart started to speed up and I shrunk. Something about his big brown eyes looking through me sent the butterflies in my stomach to war. I tried to be cool and asked about the game they were playing—mainly how much longer it would last. I also wanted to shower but couldn't do it with another guy in the room, since the bathroom was right there. Those were the rules. Dillan knew that I wanted to play because I wouldn't stop talking. He knew that I wanted us to be alone. And so did his friend—he was losing, and it was his pleasure to leave.

What happened after was an entire scene from a 1980s movie, except it was the '90s. I had no idea what I was doing and it seemed like he didn't either. We made out and started to take our clothes off and then I stopped and headed for the shower. I thought that I should clean up before doing it. He pulled me back and kissed me again, assuring me that I was clean enough. The drawer he pulled his condom from was full but I couldn't focus on that. I was in my *Sixteen Candles* moment. It was about to happen. He laid me down on his bed and gently caressed my body. We were going to make love. Then it happened and it was nothing like what I had imagined. It was painful and abrupt, and over so fast. The music that was playing in the background was loud but not enough to cover my cry. The song playing was "I Will Always Love You" by a group called Troop. Such a beautiful song during an awkward moment with two very tall people in a twin-size bed. I was flustered and embarrassed. It was me. I was a novice and couldn't do it right, that was what I immediately thought. It was a clumsy dance that was fueled by curiosity and hormones. We really liked each other and that was enough for me. When I attempted to go down on him, he stopped me. I was relieved because I had no idea how to do it. He just said, "You don't have to do that. You're my baby." Man, was I flattered by the statement, not understanding that the implication was that being a good girl meant having not-good sex. I didn't get it. I actually blushed thinking he loved me in a special way. There was blood, pain, and no orgasm. So I decided to keep doing it until I got it right.

Smells Like
Teen Parents

The summer program was over and my mom decided to come pick me up instead of letting me ride back home with the other students. She suspected that something was off with me because I wasn't answering her calls at night. It was investigation time. She had to pull me back in and regain control. The day she arrived, I had no idea she was coming. She knocked on Dillan's door. Someone must have told her that I was there. When I heard her voice, my heart started racing and my palms felt sweaty. I knew my mother—she would embarrass me anywhere in front of anyone. "I know she's in there!" she yelled from outside. "Open the door." Dillan didn't fear my mom. He was on his way to confront her, since she was banging on HIS door. I begged him to let me open it, even if it meant I would catch a beatdown in front of everyone around. Once Dillan opened the door, she walked right inside without invitation, grabbed me, and gave me a tight hug. She was aggressive and volatile and kept that energy with everyone, especially men. She ordered me to go to the car. She wanted a moment alone with my boyfriend. I went and sat in the car with my cousin and uncle, dreading what the next eight hours were going to be like. She hadn't even let me say goodbye. I looked up at Dillan's room from the rental and was afraid to even wave. A few minutes later, she sat in the van next to me and held her composure until we turned the corner. Then she jumped on me and beat me for what felt like the entire turnpike ride home. My mother had asked my boyfriend while she was up in his room if he had touched me and he looked her in the eye and told her yes. He didn't want to be dishonest with the woman he believed was going to be his mother-in-law. I really wished he would have suspended his honor and just lied. He was not the one getting slapped down the highway.

When we got home my mother ordered me not to tell a soul. She wanted me to pretend to be a virgin because my family was going to judge me and look at me differently. I was to tell no one, not even my grandmother. That wasn't happening; I told my grandmother everything. Besides, I wouldn't have to tell her. She would know. She knew me better than anyone and was understanding in how she dealt with me. She always provided me with a safe space so that I would come to her with anything. She learned from her experiences with my mother that you couldn't be too strict, that never worked.

It was a nightmare after that point. My mom would cry in the bathroom. It was as if I had died. She told me that this meant I wasn't of full value anymore and that men would know. It made me feel bad and dirty. I was no longer her little girl. She would now refer to me as a young woman and asked me grown-up questions like when I was officially getting married. And referred to my boyfriend as my husband. I wasn't ready for marriage, I just wanted to be a normal girl living a normal life. I needed fun, joy, and love. She didn't understand it because she never had it. She had so much trauma in her life that she was never really able to enjoy her youth. I felt bad about that, I loved her so much. She deserved the world.

The next few weeks only grew tenser. My stepfather knew

something was up and fished for answers, but we wouldn't break. We couldn't, he would run this into the ground if he found out. I wasn't telling him anything, besides, I never felt connected to him enough to share what was precious to me. He was opposed to me going to the program because there were too many Black people and he knew I would end up with a Black guy. My job was to find a white guy who liked me so that I could "adelantar la raza," *take the race forward.* Stupid shit Latinos say to their children since they associated whiteness with upward mobility. Little did he know that I had already given up the goods to the most beautiful Black guy on the earth. Life for the next few weeks was hard, my mom barely spoke to me. She wore her disgust brightly. I felt guilty for letting her down and most importantly my family. I was supposed to be the one that would get us out. I didn't have the stock anymore, I was damaged. But none of that really mattered to me, I was in love.

When the time came to go back to school I was feeling sick as a dog, nauseated and dizzy. I couldn't eat. My face was breaking out and I was always thirsty. I just thought I had the flu. My mother on the other hand sensed that it was something else, her biggest fear. I took a home pregnancy test and it was negative. Even though I felt like shit, the sense of relief that came over me compensated for it all.

After the relief wore off, I was back to dealing with being sick. A few days later, I took another test. I thought I was going to die when it read positive. Everything that I was told was haunting me at that moment. My life was over. I was ruined. No one was going to want to marry me. I was going to hell. All the thoughts came at me at once, along with my mother and her belt. Somehow she got a hold of the test. She was hurt, disgusted, and scared—I felt them all from her. The disappointment in her voice was haunting, she really thought that I was going to be different. I was, but she couldn't see past her rage. She hit me with her belt over and over again in the bathroom. That was the last time she beat me.

When she offered me the opportunity to fix things by having an abortion per my stepfather's suggestion, I knew that it was over for us. After years of listening to scripture and what abortion meant to my Christian family, this was my choice? I left home never to return. Dillan had threatened that he would have nothing to do with me if I had an abortion and I believed that he was all I had. I was scared, confused, conflicted, and pregnant. And the one thing I didn't have was agency over my own body and that felt suffocating. Members of my family told me to get an abortion or to go away and my boyfriend told me he would leave if I did decide to abort. It was hell! I loved him so much. I was willing to give it all up to build something with him. I truly believed he was all I had and I trusted that he would have my back.

We decided to work it out together, trying to continue school while on the brink of becoming parents. We knew that it would not be easy but what could we do? Dillan was in his first year of college football dealing with the pressure of making it to the NFL. It was common for poor kids to feel the responsibility of taking care of the family through sports. The options were limited. I was out of the house trying to go to school so that I could have a shot at a life. And still we loved each other and believed that we were going to be okay. His family was more supportive than mine. We just decided to keep going.

The day I gave birth I was in Tallahassee staying with a friend. After months of running from my mom, who was hell-bent on forcing me to have an abortion, I just stayed put. My friends were a far better support system and Dillan was there as much as he could be. My best friend, Elora, and another girlfriend rushed me to the hospital from a crab legs–filled lunch at our local Red Lobster. Dillan was supposed to be playing in his spring scrimmage game and rushed straight to Tallahassee Community Hospital from practice to meet us. I was in labor for eleven hours, naturally—Dillan didn't believe in medication. I agreed, I had no idea what I was doing. The doctor didn't help either. I already felt judged by him since he had made a comment about my pelvic bone not being developed at one of my appointments. He wasn't warm. He looked at us with pity and judgment all rolled up in one.

But he couldn't ruin one of the best days of my life—the day that my baby boy was born. Seeing him for the first time gave me hope and filled me with love. I knew that he was going to be special. I didn't know how, but I knew that we were going to be fine. It was a relief to have Dillan there. He was going to be around. He was so excited about the birth of his son, he cried when he held him for the first time. I felt that even though I had my baby out of wedlock, I had created the family I always wanted. The need for my real father dissipated and the focus became my son and his father—something about them that filled the void. Even if my own family was not a part of this, I had something else now. I had my baby and his daddy.

Dumb Bitch

I grew up listening to Spanish music. It was all that played in my house my entire life until my uncle Davie turned sixteen and introduced me to hip-hop. Prior to that, all I heard was salsa, merengue, and boleros. Héctor Lavoe, El Gran Combo, or any of the Puerto Rican greats made up the soundtrack of my childhood. I loved that music. The dialect was like mine, and I knew the words. Those were our stories. Then Davie began sprinkling in some Run DMC and Sugar Hill Gang for balance. It was my uncle Raymond who introduced me to sketch. I knew what stand-up was because of my uncle Davie, but this was different. We watched *I Love Lucy*, *The Carol Burnett Show*, and *Mama's Family*. Funny women everywhere and he loved it just as much as I did.

It was at school that I got introduced to R&B music by my friends. I would take a charter bus and the driver played the radio loud. It was as if he was drowning us out. I couldn't blame him, the bus was a circus. I was in middle school at the time and we couldn't sit still.

Through hip-hop and R&B I first heard the phrase "dumb bitch," aka a woman who was considered foolish for being the victim of the games that men played. Or at least looking back that is my own personal definition. Respectability politics at its finest. It was a term that was loosely used in the neighborhood to describe weak women, those who were victims and were being treated poorly, who didn't do better because they couldn't.

In apartment 2 lived Vicky, a Haitian woman from New York who spoke English, Spanish, French, and Creole. She had finished school and married a Puerto Rican, Amaury, the love of her life, and they had two kids. Their little girl, Sophia, looked like a mini Mariah Carey. He was a longshoreman who worked on the docks of Miami Beach. She was a nurse who was taking time off to care for her new baby. Her man was a cokehead and a cheater, often dipping into apartment 4 to get head from the resident crackhead who did enough to keep her rent paid. This was no ordinary crackhead. Lizette was a six-foot-two Afro-Cuban woman who, despite her habit and lifestyle, always had men trying to get with her. These two carried on their affair until Lizette tested positive for a baby, which she kept, figuring she could get ongoing money as opposed to the mark-up price she would declare for an abortion. From that point forward, Amaury's objective was to get his family the hell out of the building. Till then, Lizzy had the upper hand because he did everything to see to it that Vicky never found out about his extramarital baby. I knew everything because I would babysit that baby in exchange for sneakers and pants that were long enough for me. And one day, while Lizette was telling my mother about her latest exchange with Amaury, she called Vicky a dumb bitch. She laughed and laughed hard, poking fun at the wife of the man she was seeing and saying that she was the dumb one. As if she was getting over on the other lady because she, too, had a child from this loser of a man.

I started to look at womanhood as being weak and vulnerable, and I didn't want to be like that. I didn't want to be a dumb bitch, and I told my friends as much.

After all the stuff I constantly heard about women, I became quieter as I headed for eighth grade. I wouldn't even tell my uncles if someone did something to me anymore because of what it would imply about me. It would be my fault if they beat somebody up or if they killed somebody. "Never be a troublemaker. Don't start anything with a man. Don't hit a man because if he hits you back, it's your fault. Even if a man is being abusive to you, just take it. Don't be disruptive." So much of the messaging I received directly pointed to the definition of a dumb bitch. Just listening to that kind of stuff was confusing for someone like me, who was also being taught by college-educated women, who had some semblance of progressive thinking.

I had an English teacher who was a feminist, she didn't wear panties to school nor shave under her arms: Ms. Kirshner. She was fascinating. She introduced me to Toni Morrison and other great authors. To hear that women were responsible for the ills that men committed on us was just something that was starting to awaken not just the womanist in me but my humanity. I strived to understand how women had been wronged and accused of so much. I mean, even the Bible said that sin was introduced because Eve tempted Adam. I'm sure that there was more to that story than what was given to us, but it was much easier to tell us that we were responsible for tempting humankind into sin. We were also responsible for our own rapes and abuse, guilty for not wanting to take it. Everything was basically our fault and we were kinda all dumb bitches.

The girls who got pregnant: "Man, look, she's pregnant, that's a dumb-ass bitch. She knows he's going to go to college and will forget about her. Why did she do that?"

Then there was: "Look at this dumb bitch. She knows that man is married and he's not going to be there for her. Why would she do that?"

Or this: "Oh man, look at this dumb bitch. She cursed at him and he punched her in the face and she called the police, and now he's in jail because of her."

The dumb bitch phenomenon kept growing and I started to question the women in my own family. Were they dumb bitches too? Because according to the street doctrine, the answer was a resounding yes. I couldn't accept it. I was fighting against this thinking at a very young age, just understanding that what was happening to my mother and my grandmother was not okay and it wasn't their fault. Why wasn't the accountability on the culprits of the act? Why were the women always responsible for tempting somebody into doing something wrong? I just know that if somebody cut you off and you shot them, you couldn't tell a judge that the other person made you do it. I mean you could, but you probably would not get off. There was no way to use your anger to justify that action. So, why was it okay to blame women for their own abuse? Even have a term for it.

"Dumb bitch" soon became the foundation of my rebellion. I was called disrespectful, I talked back. The mousey me slowly disappeared and the young woman who started to speak up for herself and for what she thought was right began to show up. I joined speech and debate in school and began to do a lot of research and a ton of reading. This also exposed me to other schools, which meant I got to interact with many different people, including students who were in different neighborhoods, different districts. I was learning through our exchanges, not just the debates, but going to lunch and recess and having social time with these people and understanding that there was a world bigger than mine, outside of mine. I wanted to explore the beyond.

Debate was the one place that I could beat boys, and even though I could feel the contempt when I won, I loved every second of it because I was actively defying this dumb-bitch syndrome at every turn.

To all the dumb bitches out there, because I think we've all been a dumb bitch at some point: What made you that in the first place? Often, we were blamed for our own circumstances. We were demonized just because we wanted to be.

The last time I won a debate, I beat this young white man from one of the best schools in Miami. He wore a designer suit while I wore a makeshift suit and grocery store bought sneakers. I had walked to school that day in the heat. I had to prepare at the public library because I didn't have the tools at home. I did all the research without glasses, which I needed, because I couldn't afford them. I had a peanut butter and jelly sandwich for lunch with no snack. Yet I had to show up to that Lincoln-Douglas debate on abortion regardless of what my circumstances were, and I won that day. I did it for women. With all that he had and all that he came with, I still beat him. That was the moment I solidified that I was no one's dumb bitch.

The Draft

When I moved to the West Coast I spent a lot of time alone. Baby Daddy was in training camp and I knew no one in San Francisco. I would ride along the freeways and the coast and just marvel at the beauty that was California. It was only me and Baby O in the back seat listening to hip-hop, killing time until Daddy was done. Baby Daddy and I would talk on the phone until he went to sleep and I would visit him during his breaks during the day.

We were in love but we were young. We got married on a whim during his team's bye week, driving to Vegas and knocking it out in two days. My body fought it until the end—I even walked down the aisle with a fever. But it was done. And Baby Daddy and I loved each other hard. We were young and strong minded. We had arguments and made up like everyone else, there were so many layers to our love. During his off time, we read and cooked as a unit. He and my baby were my world and at the time, I sensed we were going to be alright. But then there was that feeling I had when he proposed that kept tugging at me and reminding me that this was not going to last forever. I wanted the family. It legitimized me. Even with the wives on the team, I was treated differently when I crossed over from being a girlfriend to a wife. Everything around me supported that I did the right thing. Everything except my gut.

Then Baby Daddy said, "I want you to give me a little girl. You have your boy now give me my girl!" Little did he know that she was already on the way. I was pregnant and I hadn't told him yet. I had a little PTSD from how the last one went and needed a moment to process. I had been planning to go back to school now that my son was a little older, but life had other plans and this baby was real. She came with all the frills: morning sickness, swollen ankles, strange cravings, and immediate weight gain. We had money now, but Baby Daddy was still gone most of the time.

Swept into NFL world, Baby Daddy was beginning to show signs of his past ways. He now had money, popularity, access to celebrities, and Hollywood—Los Angeles was right up the street—but he still lacked the maturity to handle it all. He became very caught up in the world and I became a liability. The pregnant wife was now a burden to someone who wanted to be part of the in-crowd. I felt like I was holding him back, and he didn't seem ready for family life. He only insisted on it because he didn't want to lose me, but it wasn't the life he really wanted. He wanted to be out with beautiful women and partying with his teammates. Meanwhile, I was at home making potpies and teaching my son how to write. I wasn't fucking ready for it either, but those babies hadn't asked to come here. I had to show up and be the mom they needed. That was what I had signed up for. When my Akaylah was born, again, Baby Daddy was getting ready for the season. He was there in the delivery room, he cried when he first laid eyes on the little girl he asked me for. But I knew that this time was going to be harder because I was thousands of miles away from the friends who held me down during my first pregnancy. And pro football season was way more intense than I was used to. My one real friend was Diann, whom I spent the six weeks of summer training camp with.

I became active with the team and their community services. I hoped that maybe I could be a part of something. I didn't feel like I had much purpose. I loved my two kids, they were my everything, but I also needed a life. Especially since my husband was running around LA with his friends pining over actresses. I needed something to do. I volunteered with the team and started to involve myself more with the charities. I wasn't a comedian yet but I was definitely the funniest wife in the bunch. I couldn't stand some of those bitches, they were mean girls. I had jokes for days, mainly picking on the other women. I wanted to humble them because I felt small in their presence.

While at a fashion show to benefit the homeless in the city, I met a TV news anchor named Lisa who had also hosted one of our fashion shows. She was genuine and grounded and nothing like the wives who had shunned me, we became fast friends. Now I had two friends. In the meantime, Baby Daddy's infidelity became more apparent and I honestly was losing interest in him. It was a relief that he was elsewhere. I preferred to be with my friends, they had my back. He started to disappear on the weekends, which meant the kids and I would have more time with our friends. They both had kids that were close with mine.

I retreated and just took care of my children. Feeling financially trapped and powerless—by then, Baby Daddy was in charge of all the finances—I started modeling again, I worked at a bank, and I became an event planner, whatever I could do to make money. I had to prepare myself for life without him, I knew it was coming. My grandmother always reminded me to have my own stash. "You can't trust a man."

She was right, Baby Daddy finally pushed me away. He had become involved with a woman in LA who was calling my home. We had barely been married a year and we had a four-year-old and a six-month-old. I could not understand what was happening. When I confronted him, he told me that he wanted a woman who had a life. That day I decided to get one.

I worked for a few months and saved my money before I left

California and went back to Florida. He didn't protest, it was as if he wanted me to leave. I was young and proud, and even though I hurt, I wasn't sticking around for more. My mother took me in with my two children and never said a word. She knew that I needed help and she just gave it to me. She offered to watch them while I looked for work, I did not want my children in the hands of a stranger. As toxic as she could be, she was a good caretaker. It was important to me that my kids were in a safe place while I tried to do the things that I needed to do to make a better life for us. She wanted to make it right between us, she was trying to be better.

Six months at my mom's and I got a job at a record label in Miami. I had been there enough and she had three kids in the house. My kids were getting used to my stepfather's screaming and I am pretty sure that they would slip them pork when I wasn't watching. We didn't eat pork, I was a recovering Seventh-day Adventist and their dad was Muslim, it was not allowed. It was time for me to go.

I talked my way into being the assistant general manager of an independent label and I actually was doing a good job. Fortunately for me, my boss was very understanding and created a space in my office for my kids while I was at work. They had a place where they could play or do homework. They were right there with me.

I got a place in central Miami, which was about fifteen minutes away from my mom. I was starting to feel my feet again. I bought my first car with my own money, furnished my place, and was able to save money. Baby Daddy had been cut from his team and decided to come to Miami after settling things in California. He sold his car and furniture and had to close out accounts. He wanted us to get back together again. I was finally finding my independence and just wanted to keep moving forward. He moved in with me and we tried again, this time it was worse. I was resentful and started talking to someone else, a guy named Jackie that I had met through the work that I was doing, he was a football player also and owned a record label. For years we had just been friends, he and I talked, and it was refreshing to chat with someone who listened.

I didn't feel bad, even though it wasn't right. I had already checked out. Baby Daddy would leave for weeks and go to Ohio to be with his football friends. They kept these houses where they gambled and partied and Lord knows what else. I was at home working, being a single mother. I had a right to some attention. I was honestly tired of it all and just not brave enough to end it. No matter how messed up Baby Daddy treated me, the thought of hurting him broke me. I continuously fell for him even though he disappointed me time and time again. I didn't feel like I could get out. One time, he came back from one of his trips and decided he wanted to try again at having a family. Although I had checked out, I decided to give it one more shot for my kids. Leaving their dad meant I was taking away from them what I had longed for my whole life. I had to try again, and try I did. But when I needed him to help with the kids so that I could work, he wouldn't. He was trying to build a business and wanted to put all his time in that. He didn't want to get a job because he felt it was beneath him: "That is for a regular person." I honestly was just tired of his bullshit.

I was thinking about getting a divorce, finding a life outside of him, meeting somebody else. I had met other people who were interested in me at the time and I couldn't believe it. I had two children and my mom told me that it would never be serious. Men didn't take single mothers seriously.

I just didn't want to be in it anymore. So, I kept moving from one place to another and he kept following me because my mom kept telling him where I was. Finally, he moved back in with me under the lie that he was going to get his own place and was just waiting for it to be ready. That was never going to happen because he gambled every dollar that he got. After a short while, it began to get ugly. There were arguments and name calling and pushing and shoving in front of our kids. I wasn't that girl that he could run game on anymore and that made him furious. He went as far as telling my mother that I was a call girl. She believed him and called me to chastise and berate me. There was constant conflict and chaos. Gone were the days of getting along. The more he pulled for me, the more I pulled away. At this point, I was the one who felt like he was heavy. I was working, I was doing everything I needed to do to take care of my family, and he was gallivanting about trying to be a designer and not wanting to get a regular job to help me financially. I just couldn't take it anymore, and that's when I decided to move back to California. I knew that he hated it there and would not follow. Nevertheless, I never disclosed where I was going.

Baby Daddy always believed that I was going to be there because I had always been there. I didn't know any better. I always counted myself last because I never took time to see the person I had grown into, the "me" that was relentless and hardworking, the survivor who did what was needed to take care of her babies. I forgot to bet on myself. After years of watching my mother and grandmother forsake themselves, I had accepted that as the way, and it was not. And I was done with it all. Whatever was going to happen would be based on my decisions not the needs of others. I was going to move to Los Angeles to pursue my dream of acting and writing and there was nothing anyone could do or say to talk me out of it. I was my own first round draft pick, finally.

Phone Boning

Throughout my elementary years, my grandmother would wait for me after school every day. I would get home, do my homework, and rush across the street to her building. I lived in 3130, she lived in 3109. Our ritual was simple: first, I would eat, she always stashed my plate away so my uncles wouldn't find it. And then we would go to her bathroom. She'd sit me down on the toilet (top down) and brush my hair, which was usually tangled after my long, active day at school. This was our time. She would check in, ask me about my day and if anything weird had happened. The women in my family were hyper paranoid about molestation, she wanted to prevent it from happening to me, but it was too late. I never told her. She continued to do the bathroom ritual until I was fourteen.

My grandmother used to go to Puerto Rico every December for as long as I could remember. She would visit our motherland right before the Christmas holidays and get back to us just in time for Nochebuena (December 24), our Christmas. Her favorite thing was to bring back food from Puerto Rico that was impossible to find in the States, like pana, and the things you could find but were better on the island, like pasteles, alcapurrias, mangos, and avocados. Something about Puerto Ricans and Dominicans going back to the islands felt ritualistic. A once-a-year visit was a reminder that they still belonged to their people, remained connected to the authentic culture, and were planning their great permanent return. I hated when my abuela left, though. I'd count the days until her return not just because I missed her but also because she was the one I would run to whenever I was being mistreated at home. When my stepfather got out of line, she had no problem reminding him that she was near and ready to shoot. She kept that .38 Special pistol with her at all times, and I knew she wouldn't hesitate to use it, she owed him. I also didn't believe it would have been her first time.

Around the time I was about to graduate from high school my grandmother had just returned from a trip to the island, a rare springtime trip outside of her holiday routine. She was so eager to see me, she called for me as soon as she got home. My grandmother was never too excited about anything so this made me want to get over there even more. Plus, I wanted to see her. So I rushed over to 3109. My grandmother's apartment building, the clean one, was always so quiet and still. She rented to older tenants to keep it that way. Something as regular as running up the stairs would stir up a commotion, causing the nosey lady from apartment 3, Doña Marta, to poke her head out of her door to see what was going on. She was an older Cuban lady who was part of my grandmother's friend group. When she popped out all you could see was her jet-black hair and blue eyes. I just waved and moved along to get to my abuela. I only knocked once, and she immediately opened the door and pulled me in for the warmest hug, followed by what felt like a thousand kisses all over my face. I could tell that she missed me too. I walked into her famously hot kitchen, where there was always a pot of Bustelo on the stove and bananas as the table's centerpiece. "Siéntate," she said pointing to a chair for me to sit down. This felt like serious business.

The rocking chairs on the balcony were for shooting the shit, but the kitchen table called for an eye-to-eye, come-to-Jesus talk. I immediately panicked thinking she was going to tell me something about her health. I was the one who would go to her doctor's appointments with her. I knew that she wasn't in the best shape. I rounded up all my vivid thoughts and my imagination took off. *Did she have some illness that I didn't know about and was going to break the news to me now? Was she dying and moving back because she wanted to die in her homeland?* Before I could go further, she smiled warmly, softening the moment, and then handed me an envelope. It was a graduation card signed, "Tus padrinos," your godparents. No additional note, just their names, Billy y Sumel, and a five-hundred-dollar check. I had no idea who these people were. I had heard about them before, but since my baptism, which I don't even remember, I never had any contact with them. My grandmother went back on one of her trips to the island and coincidentally ran into them after fifteen years. She was happy because my godmother had been her best friend at one point. Now she could introduce me to them and get me closer to the pieces of me that I was searching for. Everything about my baby days had been a mystery. There was only one picture I took with my grandmother during my big baptism party. The other pictures I had access to were of me starting at age four. And so, here was my lovely grandmother trying to help, as always.

It was a sweet interaction with them. Honestly, they are lovely people. We had a couple of phone calls and some answered questions for a few months. But the biggest question of them all was always answered with disappointment. No one knew where my father was, they had not heard from him since the 1980s. I didn't feel connected to these people, didn't know if I wanted to be. They hadn't been around, so getting to know them felt like work. It also made me feel weird to know that my mom was fifteen and surrounded by all these people who were so much older than her. That pissed me off. Being angry wasn't going to change anything in the past, or the future, because I didn't have plans to stay in touch. But here we were, time had passed and I really felt like my godparents were trying to express love mixed with regret for losing touch with their only goddaughter. It was a kind gesture but eventually our communication faded.

The last few years that my abuela went on her December trip was during the time I was living in San Francisco. I was married to Baby Daddy and we had already had our two kids. I went back to Miami to visit often. She hadn't been back to the island in a while. I assumed that it was a money issue. This moved me to work harder and make my own money. I always wanted to get rich so that I could take care of her. During one of my visits home, my grandmother invited me to come watch la novela, the soap opera, with her. When I was a kid, after she brushed my hair on the toilet, we would watch la novela before she walked me back home. I would lie on her bed watching the drama unfold on the screen and every now and then she'd whisper, "toma." Everything was a secret with her. Even when she spoke to me, she'd do this thing where she would pull me aside as if she was telling me a secret and then give me money or fill me in on family business. This time it was a phone number. I could see the happiness on her face but didn't quite get it. And then it hit me: she had found my father. It was his phone number.

I didn't know what to say. It was the moment I thought I had been waiting for my entire life and then it just went flat. I backed away from it drenched in fear. What next? I honestly didn't know how to feel. I was a little mad that she managed to find him.

When I asked how she found him, her answer prompted a realization for me about how much adoration I really had for this woman. No matter how I felt about him, it made me love her more. Instead of going to Puerto Rico the last couple of years, she had started traveling to the Dominican Republic. That is why she wasn't bringing the pana anymore, and honestly I would have preferred that more. It was that gift you didn't ask for, but you kinda did. My grandmother went to my father's homeland on her landlady pay searching for him. She walked around stalking and interviewing strangers in Santo Domingo and kept going back until she found someone who knew him. That was the ultimate act of love. I was grateful for her.

A random man named Luis, whom she met in the capitol, told her he knew who my father was and directed her to the neighborhood where he usually saw him. She headed that way. All the searching and wondering came down to this moment, she was close. When she got to the area Luis had mentioned, another man told her that my dad no longer lived there. She left her number with this man and asked him to give it to my father if he ever ran into him. It took a year, but the man eventually crossed paths with my father and gave him my grandmother's number. Now, as she handed me this number, I could tell it was a big moment for her. She had given her favorite granddaughter something that was larger than life: the connection to her father. The Dad that I had been longing for and asking about since I could talk.

My reaction was one that not even I expected. I was furious and ungrateful. I forgot how much I wanted to find him and immediately questioned why it had to happen this way. Why didn't he find me? Was he not searching for his baby girl? Did he forget about me in his new life with other kids and just cut his losses? I had so many questions but I didn't want to even think about him answering them for me. I wanted to be upset; I felt justified. Why did I have to call him? He should have been the one calling. He should have been the one looking for me.

It was a conflict in my head. I had talked so long about finally finding my father and now I was mad that he didn't find me. I wanted to jump on a plane and go find the one person that I said I wanted to know my whole life but now I felt he had given up looking for me. This made me not want to ever contact him. I couldn't forget about all the years he wasn't there. All the terrible things that happened to me, all the tears I cried. What? I was supposed to just get on the phone now and have a bonding moment when all I wanted to say to him was "Where the fuck have you been?"

Seven weeks passed, and I thought about it every day. Staring at that piece of paper, punishing myself because I really wanted to reach out. But every time I got close, I couldn't bring myself to make the call. I was stuck between pride and anger. I was afraid to learn about the life he built without me. It hurt to know that he had moved on.

I was now married to a man who did bother to give me his name and I had my two babies—they were everything to me. I also had a life far away from the people who hurt me and anyone in my immediate family and really had to consider if I wanted to disrupt that. Was I ready to bring anyone else into my world? Quite honestly this now felt more like an obligation and a burden than a possible happy reunion. I was very reluctant to engage. I just didn't know if I was ready to forgive and move on and create space for this situation. Why now? I wasn't struggling anymore, my life was good and it felt wrong to interrupt it for someone who had never been there for me.

I had to battle this onslaught of thoughts and emotions before I could actually even consider calling. I avoided my grandmother for months after that because I didn't want to make her feel bad after all that she did for me. I was missing her, not talking to her was killing me. This carried over into the resentment I had for him.

And finally, it happened. I woke up one day feeling emboldened and ready for my answers. It was like jumping in a cold pool of water: I had to get through it. As the phone rang, my mind began to race again. *Why am I calling this man?* And then a male voice said, "¿Aló?" It was him! My heart dropped. A voice that I didn't know penetrated so deeply, I wanted to cry but I just couldn't. His voice was soothing, a little raspy, not at all the super deep, masculine voice I had imagined. When I asked if I could speak to Max, there was silence. Out of nowhere I started wailing. He knew it was me. "My Kuki, que Dios te bendiga." And for just one moment my anger took a seat. I had never been a father's anything, and right now I was his Kuki. That was the moment I realized how much I really missed having a daddy in my life. I had to put everything else down and let this sink in.

The first conversation was very topical. He asked about my

mother and relatives and I shared the losses of my uncle Carlos and great-grandfather. He told me about my other siblings, who were all nearby listening in on our exchange. They were celebrating in the background, which made it even weirder. All of them knew about me and I had no idea who any of them were. All additional conversations were the same: basic questions, awkwardness, and an eagerness to end it.

We continued to talk after that, but our conversations were infrequent, I wasn't ready to commit. It was overwhelming and I couldn't just pretend that everything was okay. He was in the moment, I was in the past. I wanted to hear remorse, an apology. He was happy that he found me, I was sad that it had to happen this way. I couldn't get past my feelings so I decided to cut off communication with him and go on with my life. It was just too much for me and I was not equipped to deal with it. I changed my phone number and tried to move on as if nothing ever happened because in my mind, nothing really did.

The Mother of It All

One of the things that I've never talked about is how this reunion with my father affected my mother. From the moment my grandmother found my father to the moment I began to mull over the idea of having a conversation with him, I couldn't help but to feel guilt. It was as if I was betraying her, since she was the one who had stuck around. Why would I give an audience to the person who never tried to find me? I needed to clear it with her before I made any moves. So I called and asked her permission and how she felt about me communicating with my father after the things she had experienced when she was back in the Dominican Republic with me. She actually discouraged me from being in touch with him because she felt that I was setting myself up for heartbreak. That was what she knew from him and that was what she believed he would end up doing to me as well. She didn't believe in who he said he had become: a family man. All she knew was cheating, lies, and abandonment.

Despite what she told me and how she felt, I had to go off and see for myself. She fought it the entire time. Yet, when I decided to go see him in June 2021, she finally gave me her blessing.

I questioned her motivations because I also felt that she infected me with animus toward my father. Their relationship as man and woman had nothing to do with me. Despite whatever happened between them, I felt that she should have given me the opportunity to make that choice for myself. Instead of taking it all away when she left and allegedly kidnapped me. To be clear I don't believe that she took me away from him to punish him. I think she was seeking refuge from a person she thought was bad for her and could be bad for me. She was just taking cover and protecting her child. But she had still taken something away: my father.

In 1995 my mother went to check out a salsa band in Miami. My father was in the band, she had no idea he was going to be there. They saw each other and neither of them made an effort to talk. They were too proud and angry to connect for the sake of their own daughter. I was fuming when my mother told me about this encounter. She knew how much I wanted to find him but her personal spite didn't allow her to consider me at the moment. She partied that night, hung out with her friends, and came home as if nothing major happened.

She casually told my brother, China, the next morning and he immediately told me. We jumped in the car and sped over to that club trying to get any information we could on the band. Unfortunately, they had returned to the Dominican Republic the following morning, that's what the owner told us. I was so close and now he was gone again. I was mad at my mother for a while. It was no secret that I wanted this my entire life, she saw me cry over not having him. She read the stories I wrote about fatherhood, and knew that I felt less than around my brother and sister who had their dad. She could have given me a chance to meet the person that I wanted to meet most in the world, the chance to ask the questions that had been haunting me for years. I also had feelings about the fact that she didn't have any communication with her own father and claimed that she had no desire to meet him. I felt that she was making the same decision for me.

Perhaps when I did reconnect with him, she was a little bit jealous that I had actually found my father. My mom was never able to evolve past her own worst trauma—her own childhood molestation. She operated from that place when she was angry. She had another kid before me that she lost at birth. She'd been raising children her whole life. She raised her own children and as the second oldest one, she also helped raise her five siblings. In addition to her own past, she carried a heavy load of resentment toward my father and his family. They treated us badly when we were in the DR. So now that they had an interest in me, she was afraid that they just wanted to take advantage of me. There was also that maternal instinct that kicked in. Still, I was very upset that she had made all these decisions for me. I was a legal grown-up at this time. I already felt vulnerable, but this hit like a full-on rejection.

In 1997 when my grandmother gave me my father's number, that was the first time I had heard anything of him since I was a baby. It had taken me a minute to decide to connect with him and I really wanted to keep my mom connected to this journey. It wasn't easy. I already knew how she felt about me meeting him because she had recently had the opportunity to make that happen and didn't. Still, I wanted to bring her in. I wanted her to know that I had respect for her and that she was safe. I didn't want to do anything without including her. Even if she was a silent partner, she would know what was happening. I wanted her to feel empowered.

My father was eager to talk to me because his mom was close to death and he wanted me to come see her in the DR—he said it was her dying wish. She had diabetes and recently lost her arms and legs and was in a wheelchair. As a sign of respect to my mom, I decided to bring her into the conversation. She agreed to play nice.

I wanted to have a conversation with my parents since they were supposed to be the adults in the situation. I thought we could talk it through and possibly figure out something. This could be the chance for me to meet my father but also my grandmother, whom I couldn't remember. I arranged a conference call with them both, my mother in Miami and my father in Santo Domingo.

When I connected them, the sparks immediately began to fly and not in a good way. My father just said hello and my mother started to go off. It was flames. And by flames, I mean fire. They both felt indignant and continued to talk over each other. They just argued about who was wrong. They were both in the most selfish place of having this first-time interaction since their separation many years ago, but without any consideration for me. I felt it might have been the one common theme in their relationship.

We had only been on the call for a minute or so but it felt like forever. I interrupted. I asked my father to please explain to my mother what was happening with his mother so that we could see if I could possibly go visit before she passed away. I had no pictures of her, no recollection of any of my interactions with her or any of my family in the Dominican Republic. I was interested and curious to see what this could mean for me in terms of reconnecting with the other side. My father's response to my prompt was to accuse my mother of kidnapping me, and her comeback was about his affair with a white woman. I had to scream and interrupt again. He told her, "You took her away from me. I didn't have any contact with her. Her last name isn't even my last name." Her response was: "Her last name has never been your last name. You gave it up for a welfare check." She maintained that my father didn't sign my birth certificate so that they wouldn't lose their state benefits. And the bickering started again. Finally, I had to scream at the top of my lungs, "Stop, stop, stop! You may not believe this, but this conversation is not about either of you. It is about me!" My grandmother was close to death. We didn't have a lot of time. Yet they had hijacked the call and made it about themselves. I suddenly saw point-blank the lack of consideration and respect these two people had for each other.

"I want her to come here. My mother is near death and it is very important. Her dying wish is to see the granddaughter she hasn't seen since she was a baby," argued my father. I was only told negative things about my grandmother, but at this point it was only from my mother. As I was getting older, I was learning that she too was flawed and had the potential to lie. She had been hurt by a man that she loved, who betrayed her. There was a real possibility that she and my grandmother didn't see eye to eye, but that had nothing to do with how my grandmother felt about me. Up until this point we had never been separated, we had always been a unit. Seeing it from my perspective, all the feelings toward my mom were also toward me. That was not how it worked. I was my paternal grandmother's flesh and blood, the first daughter of her beloved son. My mother was a girl that he dated. My mother hated this woman, she hurt her deeply. But my father was the one responsible for it all. He should've stepped in and been a man. Meanwhile, I was stuck in the middle, and it was hard to know what was true versus what was real. Because what could have been real for my mother was her perception, but the truth was absolute. My grandmother could have very well loved me and never had the opportunity to show it. I didn't know any of this for certain, but it was definitely going through my head.

"Absolutely not. I don't think it's a good idea," replied my mother. "Your mother never gave a shit about her when she was a baby. Why does she care about her now? She threw us out of the house repeatedly."

"She threw you out of the house, not her," quipped my father. That sounded completely crazy to me. How could you throw my mother out of the house and try to keep her baby? It was all so confusing, hurtful, and toxic I honestly just wanted it to stop. I could not believe how he was carrying on. He was still trying to put her in her place by making her feel bad.

"Well, where do you think she was when I was out on the street? She was with me, her mother. Did you really think I would leave my daughter in that house?" said my mother. I could hear the pain in her voice, it was as if this had just happened. Neither of them had let it go.

"Well, you could have left her in the house with my mother," he replied. And at this point, I started to fade. This was going nowhere fast and it honestly was exhausting. I just wanted to be done with both of them by this point.

"Absolutely not. Your mother was a bad person, she raised you. She wasn't kind. Why would I leave my baby with a person who is capable of throwing a baby's mother out of the house?" said my mom. And they were back at it again, almost two minutes later.

"Margarita, my mother is dying," he said, in a pleading voice. "They have cut her arms and her legs off."

"They should have cut her head off," replied my mom without missing a beat. Right then and there, I knew there would never be a resolution when it came to these two. They started arguing again. I hung up the phone and I began to cry. I remember thinking, *Why and how did I end up with two fucked-up parents?* I understood then that these two people who were responsible for bringing me into this world would never grow up, and I would always have to be the adult in a conversation with them.

In the end, I decided not to go to see my grandmother because I felt like it would just cause too much conflict with my mother. Honestly, I didn't have the support, and emotionally, I didn't feel equipped to take that trip to the Dominican Republic by myself to meet a woman who had, from what I understood, been so mean to my mother. I just had to let it go.

That was right around the time I decided to let my father go again because I felt that him being a part of my life was going to be too complicated and cause too much dissent and conflict with my mother. My mother was the one parent who stayed, and regardless of how messed up it might have been, she didn't leave me. In my mind, that was enough. I just accepted that as a gift. I loved my mother and honored her for being present. I don't feel the same now, I think it's healthy to hold your parents accountable and take your space. You don't owe them your sanity and peace of mind. They chose to have you. I do believe in respecting them, but I also appreciate the point of view that we all have to earn respect.

I never got an apology from my mother. She never said, "My bad, that wasn't cool. I should have stayed out of it. You should definitely meet your father." She, in fact, doubled down when I told her that

I was going to stay away. "Good for you," she said. "You should stay away from that man. He is not good for you." And for many years, I did stay away because I didn't want to upset her. I didn't want her to feel betrayed. I also felt that he probably wasn't good for me. After all, he was awful on that call too. He never went on a mission to find me. He actually came to the United States to play gigs, but there was no evidence of him actively searching for his child while he was here. He never reached out to my godparents, his friends, anyone to find me. (They did.) It was very complicated. I was also very distraught about the whole situation because deep, deep down inside, I wanted my father. I wanted to know who he was. When I finally had talked to him, I wanted more. The fact that my mother wasn't in support of that and actually condemned it weighed heavily on me.

In 2007 one of my sisters found me on Facebook. My opening joke on *Last Comic Standing* was about how that made me unique and a star. Roseanne Barr cackled and asked me why I didn't have my own TV show yet.

My sis Rhada knew that I had pulled away previously but wanted to have her own relationship with me. I was in a different place from before. I was now living in LA, on the verge of starting stand-up, and I welcomed the idea of reconnecting with my family. I had decided at this point that I was going to meet him one day to talk to him in person. I needed his version of the story, his why, to explain the things he did. I didn't want either of us to pass away without an embrace I could remember.

I also wanted to connect with my siblings. I found out through Rhada that my little brother had met a woman from Los Angeles and was getting married and then moving here. I was ecstatic about the possibility of an in-person connection with him. At the end of the day, we were all victims in the whole situation and I didn't hold them responsible for any of it.

I started to communicate more but it was on and off. I had trust issues. There were times when I was all in, and I felt very excited, hearing the stories, talking with them, feeling a part of something.

Even though it wasn't in person. My mother was not in support of any of it. She couldn't separate anything in the Dominican Republic from my father and his mother. But I didn't care anymore. I continued to communicate with my family. I had this loving relationship with my siblings. I was intrigued by who they were, and they were intrigued by who I was. My father would try to interrupt in a paternal tone, with advice and discipline and suggestions, as if he had been there in my life all along. Then came some requests. He wanted me to help him get back to the States. Wait, but I didn't even know him.

My siblings and I decided that we were going to meet at some point. Financially, I knew that they couldn't afford to see me and at the time I couldn't either, but I knew that I would make it happen when the cards lined up. For the time being, we had WhatsApp, we talked on the phone, and I would be seeing my brother in Los Angeles in person soon too.

And then in 2019 I booked my very own HBO Max one-hour special. This was a comedy milestone. I had been working toward it for ten years. I couldn't believe it, I was ecstatic. That was the one thing I had always wanted as a comedian, my very own special. I started to prepare for it. Shooting was due to start in 2020 and then March hit and Covid brought everything to a standstill. My special was indefinitely postponed. The pandemic made us face our mortality, so I began to speak to my father more. I was worried that I might lose him before getting to see him in person. I wanted to mend my relationship with him.

When things started to ease up after the worst of the pandemic was over, the special was back on the table and the time had come to get to work. As I prepared for my taping, I knew I also wanted to show people how some comedians mine their material. I liked the idea of sharing the process and allowing them to see how a lot of the stuff we talk about comes from our personal experiences, many of which they've probably gone through too. Growing up without a parent isn't just relegated to race and culture and ethnicity, it is a global thing. I believe comedy can normalize certain situations, make people feel seen. I wanted those who supported me to get to know me more. So, although as a private person this idea terrified me, I suggested adding a documentary angle to the special, which wasn't such a big departure from my comedy, and that was inked in my deal with HBO Max. The comedy special would include shots of me in Puerto Rico and the Dominican Republic revisiting parts of my childhood and capturing the moment where I see my father again, which to me was really like meeting him for the first time. If anything, this would give me the chance to register this magical moment of me seeing him, hugging him, interacting with him for the first time in my memory. And I could have it forever.

Right before I flew to the Dominican Republic, I had the conversation with my mother again. At this point, I had made the decision that regardless of how she felt about it, I was going to go. I needed to do this for myself. It was important for me that she understood that this was going to happen with or without her. The conversation didn't go so well. Aside from being bothered by the whole thing, for the last few years, she had been struggling with an addiction to painkillers she developed after a knee surgery—one of the reasons why I had stayed away from her. That addiction became a source of a lot of pain and anger for her, and me planning to see my father after she had expressed how awful of a human being he was only made everything worse. She'd already made it clear that she believed I should stay away from him. So she interpreted my need to see him again as a blatant act of defiance.

To feel that I was beholden to either of my parents was just ridiculous. The decision had been made, I just wanted her blessing, which I did not receive, but I moved ahead with the plan regardless, and it was okay because it was what I needed to do for myself and for my family. I also wanted my children to meet their grandfather and know that side of themselves as well. After being in therapy on and off for the last eight years, doing the work to heal myself, I understood that this meeting wasn't about me reconnecting with my father so that he could pick up where he left off, or he could make up for what he didn't do. It was just the decision of two adults meeting who should meet, see each other, learn about each other, know about each other, who had the opportunity to do it, who were separated against their will. And it was important to me.

So, I was going to go see my father. I was going to go meet him. I was going to have the opportunity to see the other side of me, to touch it, to feel it, to smell it, and to just be connected to it in a way that I had never been before. I had reached a different place in my life, in my adulthood where I felt like I could actually get this done and walk away from it stronger and better for it, as opposed to broken, which is what my mother feared. I'm glad that I did it because so many questions were answered and I had the opportunity to come back and deal with some real things in my own life. I decided to take therapy more seriously and became more committed to my mental and emotional health. I wanted to be a better person, woman, mother, and daughter.

Bendición, Papi

When I was eleven years old the Miami Dade County Youth Fair came to town. It was one of the big events in the city that happened in the spring and everyone I knew went, from the kids on my block and the kids at my school to my uncles with their girls. I sometimes went with my class as a school field trip. I rarely went with my family because we didn't have the money. Also, I was the only one old enough to get on the rides and that simply wasn't enough for the effort. But this particular year my mother promised me that she would take me and I couldn't believe it. I loved everything about it, from the Himalaya ride to the French fries to the picture booth. I talked about it with my friends all day at school and I couldn't focus on anything but the school day ending. My friend Laura and I even planned to meet up so that we could ride together.

That evening after doing my homework, I took my shower and got dressed for my big night. I sat on the couch in the living room waiting for my mom and stepfather to get ready so that we could go.

Instead, a big argument unfolded between the two of them about why we should *not* go. It was a weekday, for example, and I had younger siblings. All of this we already knew when we made the plan. I sat and nervously watched them battle it out hoping that my mother would finally win. She did not.

I stayed put staring at the trees through the sliding glass doors in our living room, hoping that they could tell me something. I would always ask them for the yes or no answers. It had become a practice since I was about five. One of the questions that I asked them was if my father was going to ever show up. I wanted to know if that would be the moment I could expect him. It was my first memory of imagining how meeting him for the first time would be. My mom would not have to take me to the fair because he would turn up to do it. A black limousine would pull up to the building and he would get out with flowers and a teddy bear as big as me. He would make his way to the front door and knock loud like a cop. When my stepfather answered the door, as he always did, my real father would simply say, "I am here to pick up my daughter." It was just that simple. That thought stayed with me well into my adulthood. All I wanted was for him to show up and claim me.

When I became an adult, the fantasy of how it would go when I met my dad was a very warm one. It would be as if no time had passed and we would pick up right where we left off. Lots of hugs and kisses would take place and we would be totally in sync with each other, finishing each other's sentences and laughing at each other's jokes. He would tell me what a beautiful person I had grown into and how much I reminded him of himself. And a mere interaction would answer some of the questions I had like "Why am I this tall?" and "Do you hate meat like I do?" and "Do you want to move to America?" I had more but we could start there. He would answer all of them with a big smile on his face, holding me, telling me everything that I wanted to know. The best part of the interaction would be that from that point forward we would never be separated again. But that's now how it went.

My dad and I started talking again after my divorce, we stayed in touch via phone. It was infrequent, I was still on the fence. I didn't have the opportunity to make an international trip—I was a single mom and was working to take care of my family. And he still had not made it to the States to see me, even though he was able to make trips to New York—I felt bad about that. Still, every time he phoned me and I heard him call me "Kuki" I would melt.

My brother moved to California and I wanted to meet him. He was younger and blameless in the situation. It would be an opportunity to learn about my father and his side from a neutral source. It was great, we became cool and continued our own relationship that had nothing to do with our father. He was instrumental in me wanting to go to the DR, he told me about all the other people in my family who were also a part of who I was. I had sisters, nieces, nephews, and cousins who were eager to meet me and loved me already.

Meanwhile, I had been working for twelve years as a comedian and my career was paying off. This time in a big way: I had booked my HBO Max hour comedy special, and I decided to write about and document meeting him. Comedy was my life at this point. The doc would cover me returning to the DR to meet my father and reconnect with the only other country I lived in. This piece was going to show my viewing audience just how the pieces of my life ended up in my routine. I underestimated the emotional toll this would take on me, I was just thinking about comedy.

The morning I actually saw my father for the first time was horrific, nothing went well. It was 2021, during the COVID-19 pandemic. The world was upside down and everything was filled with uncertainty. Being faced with my own mortality after watching so many people die, I wasn't taking anything for granted. But that morning, in a hotel room in the Dominican Republic, I was an emotional wreck. After weeks of not sleeping more than four hours a night, I woke up feeling vulnerable and weak that day. My sleep-deprived eyes were burning. I was also losing my voice and felt riddled with anxiety, which sparked concern about my health because I knew that the exhaustion made me vulnerable. No one could understand what I was feeling no matter how much they tried! I was a little kid again needing direction every step of the way. I had to pull myself together, but I was not ready. As I went to pull out the cotton two-piece pant set I had planned to wear that day because it was loose and cool and I needed to be comfortable, I started to cry. It was loud and deep. Years and years of wanting my father boiled down to this one moment. My children were the ones who came to my rescue, I can't imagine what that felt like for them. I was completely unraveled, shaken and even a bit destroyed. That kind of cry was not something I would do around them when they were growing up. They helped me pull it together, they reminded me who I was. Beautiful to know that they saw me in a way that I didn't even see myself. My daughter reminded me of my strength and resilience and my son highlighted my kindness and compassion. And they put me back together, moved over to the other side of the suite, and assured me they were just one call away. That was one thing that made me feel safe, my two hearts always made everything better.

While in the makeup chair, I had another mini meltdown. I looked exhausted and felt ugly. Filled with compassion, Stephanie, the artist, worked her hardest to make me look put-together and perk me up. Then there was Nadia, the director of my doc who was steadfast by my side throughout it all. We talked right before he came in and she assured me that if at any moment I felt uncomfortable, we could stop. She took my situation as if it were her own, she held me up when my knees buckled.

When I first heard the knock on the door, I shook, I could not steady my hands. I needed to open the door, something had to give. I took two deep breaths. I was including this footage in my HBO special, an added layer that made me feel even more vulnerable. Nadia assured me that it was a safe space. She was the only one who would be in the room with me, no additional crew. She and I related to each other on so many levels it was like having a family member present who just happened to be holding a camera. He lightly tapped on the door again; it was time. Now my knees were shaking too and I was queasy. When he first walked in, I froze. I honestly didn't know how to react. There was no instructional guide on how to feel when you meet your dad for the first time. As he stepped into the room, I heard his soft cries and was in shock. I could not emote. I asked him if he was going to hug me. I thought it would be his natural reaction. He waited for permission. The first hug was awkward, I grabbed his head and gave him the blessing. "Bendición, Papi," that was the first and only time I ever said that to my father. I heard so many people say it, I hoped that one day I would be able to say it to my father too. It didn't connect for me, I felt like a fraud. My father and I were strangers, that was a term of endearment. We took a seat on a couch in the suite and while words were coming out of his mouth, I couldn't shake the voices in my head. *What is wrong with you? Why are you being so cold? I thought you wanted this.* I was in another world, so much so that I didn't realize that he was still sobbing.

After those first few moments together, I was confused because pity was not something I expected to feel for my dad. I had a split second of regret for coming, all I could think of was having one more person to have to take care of. And then looking at him made me feel bad for thinking that. I was on an emotional roller coaster and I desperately wanted to jump off. Instead, I focused on my sisters and their children. They would eventually also give me insight and provide me with information that helped me learn more about our dad. I wanted their perspective; I was interested in seeing what it looked like for those who grew up with him. I thought that maybe it would show me what I would be like if I actually had grown up with him.

I met my sister Mariana that day. She stood still when we were introduced. She is also tall like me, about five foot ten, and I could see some similarities in her baby face. She greeted me softly, "Manita," and gave me a hug. I felt sincerity from her, she had a serene nature. She also felt mature, she was definitely the adult in the situation with my father. She had driven him to see me because he was living with her at the time. My father's partner had passed away a few months prior and she took care of him during his time of grief. Our meeting was short but sweet, we would see each other again the next day at lunch. I was having a meal with my three sisters, five nieces and nephews, and one husband. But for now, it was just me and my dad for the rest of the day. We were going to visit some places and meet some people. I wanted to get as much as I could in, I didn't know when I would return, the fate of the world was up in the air.

We went to the beach that he used to take me to when I was a baby, Guibia. This was the place we went to the most, he said. I loved the water when I was little, my mom would take pictures of my dad and me on the beach. I remember seeing a whole photo shoot of him with me at that beach. My maternal grandmother, Aida, had a picture of me on that beach, framed and hanging on her living room wall. As we walked side by side, my father shared other details with me, he was trying to catch me up to speed, giving me tidbits of information, attempting to cover as much ground as possible. He told me that his grandfather, who loved me very much, called me "Bobola." He said that I had an aunt who also lived in the house while I was there. Isabel was around my mom's age. She had a daughter named Aida too.

The topic of my paternal grandmother came up—the other Aida. At this point I had only been told bad things about her and not just from my mom. My siblings had confirmed that they too had heard bad things about her. But here was my father telling me that she adored me and never wanted me to leave. He said that she always waited for me to come back and that her dying wish was to see me. I had a hard time believing him, but he insisted. I was beginning to feel a bit more relaxed now. I had my kids with me and people from the crew were around us as we walked along the beach. He kept trying to find opportunities to have me to himself and I kept slipping away, I didn't trust him.

When we left the sandy shore to take him home, he asked if we could stop somewhere on the way. He wanted me to visit some people who knew me when I lived there, two ladies that I didn't remember, but apparently were a part of my village. We drove through the streets of la Zona Colonial as the tigres hung out, listening to perreo music that played so loudly we could hear it through our rolled-up windows while driving in the car. As we pulled up to this unfamiliar space, everything felt so distant from me, I couldn't even pretend that it wasn't strange and foreign. My daughter had to encourage me to step out of the car and, as I did, I was received by this overwhelming energy that despite being unknown, felt genuine and warm. These two older ladies who stood outside their apartment waiting were so happy to see me, one cried as she hugged me. "Mi Kuki regresó," she said, happy I had come back. The duo who had my mother's back during our time in Santo Domingo had been waiting for our return so much that when I stepped out of the car, they looked inside expecting my mother to follow. I didn't even catch their names because the reunion was so emotional for them that I felt bad because I couldn't reciprocate. I really didn't know these angelic women who bathed and fed my mother and me when my father went on the road and my grandmother kicked us out of the house. We slept on that beach that he used to take me to, the callejones (alleys), and in these ladies' home. So even if I didn't remember them, I felt like I owed them respect and gratitude. I wish that I did remember them, they were the sweetest, most genuine people, I didn't want to say bye. After we left, I dropped my dad off at my sister's and went back to my hotel to decompress. It had been a long day filled with a lot of people, information, and experiences that were new for me. It was the first day I had a dad.

The next morning, in addition to shooting around the places where I once roamed with my mom, I was set to meet the rest of the family. I had to emotionally prepare myself for a lot of people who always knew about me. I had spoken with these people on the phone, but meeting in person was different. There would be expectations of hugs, questions, and comparisons. I had just met my father the day before, this was a lot to take in. They were the women who had the benefit of growing up with him. No matter how hard it seemed, they had their father. Someone to call papi who was there for birthdays and special events. Two of my sisters were married, they had him to walk them down the aisle. I had an innate jealousy about these things. The only person I ever called Papi was my great-grandfather, and my son walked me down the aisle when he was barely four years old. Now that I had to face this, I really was hoping my saltiness would not be evident because at this point I was pretty raw.

My children and I met them in a hotel lobby—our Dominican family had to get tested for Covid before we could get together. They came in groups, thank God the producers did it that way. First my sister Rhada brought her daughters Jael and Azul and her husband, El Típico Dominicano, who is a YouTuber. My sister speaks fluent English, she lived in Orlando, Florida, with our aunt for some time. To think I had been right down the turnpike in Miami during that time. We were so close and yet so far, I didn't even know she existed back then. Next, my sister Mariana came in with my two nephews, Pedrito and Axel. Her husband had to work so he couldn't make it. My father was with her, he tried to make introductions. I then met my sister Tiffany and her son, Leurys. Tiffany had a different mother too, she and I are the only ones who don't have Hindu names. After everyone arrived, we began to take pictures. I took snapshots with my sisters, nieces and nephews, and every other combination possible. Standing around together, I realized they were all tall too—that's where I got my height from. My kids really vibed with their cousins and I am sure it was refreshing for them to see a reflection of themselves in family members. My daughter shared that she felt good to meet her aunt Tiffany because she had someone in her actual family that looked like her.

I never thought it would happen. Since my mom had never met her father, I didn't think I was going to meet mine. Our lunch was actually pretty good. We ate as a family and I can honestly say that it was a special event in my life. I looked around and saw everyone happy and sharing that special moment and actually forgot that the cameras were rolling. My father made a teary-eyed speech, and we then went around the table and everyone said something. I could sense some tension coming from my sister Tiffany, she seemed a bit distant from everyone. She worked her way around the table to tell me that she always felt far from the other siblings. Our father actually married the mother of his four children. One of the realities of coming to your country from the States is that the assumption is made that your life is perfect because it seems better. I was not emotionally equipped to take on other people's issues, I was trying to resolve my own. This is the Dominican family that I didn't know about until I was in my twenties, the father whom I only knew from one picture. I was far from stable myself, looking around at all these people trying to figure out what it all meant now. Was I supposed to stay in touch with all of them? Did I really want to? Part of me really didn't know if I did. Was I setting these kids up for disappointment? What was the expectation? As we wrapped up our meal, I was sobered by the realization that the next day I would be gone. This was not enough time, how was I going to leave now? There was still so much getting to know each other. I wanted to bond with the kids. Getting up from that table felt like fighting to get to the top of the pool, I needed air. I could feel the knot in my throat forming.

As we approached the exit of the restaurant, I couldn't breathe. It was just so much. I actually felt sad that I was about to leave my father. That made me erupt into tears I could no longer contain. My kids both gathered around me and held me up. They had been so supportive this entire trip, I didn't even think about how all of this was affecting them. I was such a mess and they knew it. Just as we disbanded, my father pulled me in for a hug. This was what I had been waiting for my entire life: that daddy-daughter moment when no one can console you but your very own father, whose entire mission is to comfort his baby girl and make it all better. And as I sobbed into his shoulder, he gently whispered in my ear, "I'm going to need you to give me some money." My world shattered in an instant. It was as if I had been punched in the gut a thousand times and was being forced to stand up straight just after he took the wind right out of me. I was overcome with sadness but also embarrassment, the mics were still on and the crew could hear everything. I slowly walked over to my car and just slumped right into the back seat of the SUV. I felt like a fool.

Our meeting was nothing like what I had daydreamed about for so many years. It was quite the opposite; it was awkward and weird and unfamiliar and uncomfortable. I was embarrassed and angry and sad and wanted to run away as fast and as far as I could. The pain that I had felt after spending time with him and feeling like all he saw was a meal ticket was deflating. It killed my vibe. All the build-up for over three decades immediately hit the ground like a bungee jump gone wrong.

I couldn't think outside of myself at the moment. The Aida who always put others first and gave everyone the benefit of the doubt faded. I had no desire to consider his situation, to extend empathy. He ruined my moment. It wasn't precious. It wasn't tender. That feeling of being my actual father's "little girl" would never be realized and I had to accept it. I was now a grown woman to him and a resource.

While all these thoughts and emotions rushed through me, I had to go back to the hotel and pull myself together yet again; I had a comedy show to do that evening and the people coming to see it were not responsible for anything that I was feeling. Before my performance, I sat in the hair and makeup chair once again in a daze, my eyes swollen and tired. I had bags under my eyes so deep that I looked sick. I couldn't look at the mirror in front of me. But I sucked it up and, with a heavy hand of makeup covering my eye bags, I put on a pretty dress, and headed for the stage. It was time to make people laugh. I really wanted this piece to turn out good, I was excited about showing the beautiful people of the Dominican Republic to the world. My people.

We had a great show, everyone shined. I was especially proud of the opportunity to share the stage with some of the Dominican Republic's finest comedians. After the show, I had a pizza party in my room with my sister Rhada and her family and my sister Tiffany and her son. I was seeing them one last time before I departed for Puerto Rico. I wanted to hold on as long as I could before I left the next morning. I was going to miss them. And yes, I wanted to stay in touch.

I was scheduled to wrap my documentary in Puerto Rico featuring my maternal family. By the time we landed at Luis Muñoz Marin International Airport, some of the tension from those previous couple of days was gone. I could sense this was going to be a lighter trip. Interestingly enough, though I had only been here once before, I immediately felt at home. This was the place where the people I grew up with were from and I wanted to honor them. There was my great-grandfather, Papi, whom I had the privilege of knowing and growing up with through high school, thank God for teenage pregnancy! Then, of course there was the queen, my grandmother, who raised me and my mom together and was the matriarch of our family. This was the birthplace of the love of my life, my mother and my uncle Carlos who I could never forget. And my uncle Raymond, who had taken on the role of father. He liked to tell everyone that my brother China and me were his kids, and people believed him. He felt some type of way about my other brother and sister having a dad so he stepped up and became ours. I was in their homeland and took them everywhere I went. I released them in the place that they had always wanted to come back to, "La Isla."

The last few days in my homeland enriched me in a way that I needed. I was embracing where I came from and learning more about myself as a person, as an artist. Getting more context from my people equipped me to go tell more of our stories. I wanted that to come across in this special. I visited Caguas, the place of my mother's and grandmother's birth; I danced with the locals; I ate my native food; and I visited the beach. Our comedy show in Puerto Rico was also going to feature local talent and I couldn't wait to hit that stage. I was thinking about my father but I had to stay in the moment, there was still so much that had to get done and this place was a part of me too.

Raymond

My uncle Raymond quit school the day I was born. For some reason
he knew he would be part of the reason that I would stay alive. He
was part of my parental team until he departed from this earth and
was one of the best human beings I have ever met in my life. My uncle
Raymond was always part of everything that happened in my life. One
of the things that he always wanted to do was celebrate my fifteenth
birthday, my quinceañera.

Battling with addiction since he was a teen was something that
always prevented him from having a stable life. But whenever he was
off drugs, he was always on point. He kept the job. He was really good
at everything that he did. He was very responsible, and to date, one of
my favorite parents. He was one of the most affectionate of the people
in my life, always hugging and kissing me, and used to make sure that I
ate, because I didn't like to eat. I've always battled with self-destructive
eating habits. I guess that's one of the ways I dealt with my emotional
issues.

My uncle Raymond was always there. He used to pick me up from school and walk me home. He would bathe me and feed me and take care of me, help me with my homework, watch movies with me. He was who I saw *The Sound of Music* with—and *Bambi* and *Purple Rain* and *The Wizard of* Oz and all the movies that made me believe in magic. He was just such an important and instrumental part of my life. My relationship with my uncle Raymond was very deep because I was always around and aware of all that was happening with him. My grandmother was obsessed with saving her son and I was aware of it all because I was the translator. So when it came to his addiction, she would try to clean him up at home and I was there. When that didn't work, she would send him to the crisis center and I had to make the phone call. It was hard for me to see my uncle dealing with the level of pain, such a heavy burden for me to carry as a child. Especially when I had to be the reason he would get locked up because it was me calling. I would blame myself.

With time, he became a handyman at the building that my grandmother managed and would help my mom with her kids. He helped everyone in our neighborhood when he could, not to mention my grandmother, mother, and me. I used to sleep in the bed with him when I was little. When my mom was not in a relationship, he would live with us. Raymond was probably one of the most harmless people I ever met in my life. He slept with me because I was scared of everything and thought that bad things were going to happen to me at night. He was there to make sure that they didn't because, I suspect, they had happened to him when he was a kid. The thing that made it so easy with him was that he just knew, I never had to speak of the uncomfortable, he was familiar with it.

Uncle Raymond was a queer man who was never allowed to come out because our culture is so machista, homophobic, and toxic that it was dangerous for him. Our family was also "religious," so he lived with the constant reminder that his true self was considered an abomination before the Lord. I can only imagine how difficult that must've been to process when you can't help how you feel. So he always had to present in a manly form, which he was fine with, but he also happened to be a homosexual male, which he had to keep under wraps.

As a result of some sexual abuse during his early years and not being able to live out loud, he was in a very dark place as a young adult. One day, when I was seven years old, I tried to go into the bathroom because I really had to use it and the door wouldn't open. The harder I pushed to avoid peeing on myself, the quicker I realized that something was pushing it closed. That something was my uncle lying on the floor bleeding because he had cut himself in an attempted suicide. As I stood there frozen with pee running down my legs, all I could think about was how my uncle looked like the crucified Jesus. Luckily, he didn't die and was sent to a mental facility. From that day forward, I never wanted anything else to do with a cross with Jesus on it.

My uncle was my best friend, a confidant. He was there throughout my young life. There on my first day of school, there when I graduated from elementary school. He would come to my aid when I got in trouble at school, covering for me with my mom to avoid her punishment. When I got sick at school, he would walk over to pick me up—he didn't learn how to drive until later in life, so he would always show up on foot. He was always there.

The day my period came, Raymond went to the store and bought my pads, and came back to talk me through it. I remember feeling so depressed about it. I didn't know what it meant to me yet. I had been doused with the belief that getting your period meant you were officially a virgin, a señorita, which meant you were now of childbearing age. That was all I kept hearing from my grandmother and mother. It was very confusing and complicated as a kid to hear somebody tell you that you were ready to have kids just because of a function of your body. Maybe physically you were, but that definitely didn't take your emotions and mentality into account. I was really going through it, I felt like any man I came in contact with who wasn't in my family would see me as a potential mate. That really grossed me out. But Uncle Raymond was there and he knew I wasn't ready for all of that. I wasn't ready to be a woman, I was still a kid doing kid things. I wanted to just hurry and put that damn maxi pad on so I could go outside and jump in the next kickball game. I pretended that it was not happening, I wanted to just stay a kid. And Uncle Raymond always made me feel like a little girl, his little girl. He called me his princess. Even after me having two kids and being divorced, he still called me this. It was such a gift because it's something that felt fatherlike to me. No one else called me that.

The first time I went on a date, my uncle was there. I was not allowed to have a boyfriend yet. My mom was very strict about that. So we called this a friend outing, my best friend Karen at the time joined me with her date. And my uncle had me covered because we all knew my mom was paranoid with me when it came to sex. She feared I was going to have a baby early like herself and that fear was always the driving force of how she reared me. A lot of times, it was with physical violence. But my uncle trusted me and knew who I was and wasn't afraid that I was going to get pregnant because he believed that I had a good head on my shoulders. Me liking a boy was something that I would also share with my uncle because he liked boys too. So he understood on a whole other level.

The guy's name was Tommy, my first real crush who liked me back. He was tall, skinny, and brown with hazel eyes and the biggest smile. I met him at my job. I worked at a Marketplace in downtown Miami where I fried dough. He came by one day and bought an elephant ear and asked if he could call me. I had seen him there several times and just gazed at him from afar. There was no way he was going to like the geek frying flour, but I guess I was wrong. He wanted my number but I had to take his, since I wasn't allowed to get calls. His parents were from Haiti and, like me, he spoke two languages, English and Creole. He was a great kid that had a bright future ahead of him. I knew that about him based on when we talked. He wanted to go to college, which wasn't an option for many people where we grew up. He had dreams too and we soon started to talk about them over the phone when I called him at night after my mom went to sleep. She had to go to sleep when her husband went to bed, he was that controlling. What's more, he would get up early for work and she had to be up before him to make him breakfast and see him off. Anyway, Tommy and I talked so much at night that I eventually got a second line at home using my grandmother's social security number that no one knew about except her. I kept the phone in a drawer with the ringer off. We talked so much that he eventually asked me out on a date. I was so used to just talking on the phone, I didn't know how we would make it work. I had a conversation with my dad/confidant/ uncle and he talked to my mom about it. She agreed on letting me go out with coed friends to the local amusement park so long as my uncle came along. Tommy said that he was okay with my uncle going on our first date with us if that meant that I could go. But my uncle was not going to ruin it for me, his words. He just had us drop him off and go on about our business, and then arranged for a set time to be picked up on the way back home. He lied to my mom and told her that he was there the entire time to chaperone. Tommy was older than I was, he was a senior and drove, and for some reason my uncle trusted him. I was still a virgin and hadn't even kissed a boy yet. I think there was something refreshing about me that made Tommy really like me, maybe he appreciated this halo of innocence around me and respected and honored it. I really lived in a John Hughes movie. Needless to say, we went to the amusement park to eat candy apples and cotton candy, go on the rides, play games, and did nothing that my mom imagined would happen. It was actually very sweet. He didn't make me feel like I was of childbearing age, she did. I was just a cute innocent girl to him. He actually asked me to be his girlfriend that day.

I was on cloud nine on the way home. It was the perfect night. Then we picked up my uncle Raymond on the way and he asked Tommy if he could drop him off somewhere after they dropped me off. Of course, my heart and stomach sank because I knew that my uncle was battling with addiction and Lord knows what would hap- pen on that ride. Where was he asking my brand-new, first boyfriend to take him? Tommy didn't even flinch; he said that it was not a problem. Even though I knew deep down he wouldn't cross me, my uncle held all the cards, he kept the secret, so I couldn't protest.

After dropping me off, my uncle asked Tommy to take him to the liquor store. Then he bummed ten dollars off him to buy the liquor and asked him to wait so that he could drop him off at home. Tommy did all of it and didn't think twice. When I found out about this the following morning, I thought it was the most embarrassing day of my life, but Tommy just laughed it off and never brought it up again.

I eventually laughed about this moment too because that was my uncle Raymond. Everything that riled up others about him made me want to be closer to him. I just adored him so much and I understood the circumstances of his life. It wasn't easy for him, so I gave him a pass.

A week after my first date, Uncle Raymond started talking about my quinceañera. I had my period, a boyfriend—it was time. He wanted to prepare for my coming out party, even though it was still a year away. First stop, Fingerhut, a mail-order catalog company that was popular in my hood where you could order anything from plates and bedding to furniture. My uncle Raymond was all over that. He started ordering stuff for my big event, which was the sweetest gesture, because nobody else was thinking about throwing me a party. It wasn't in the economics of my family and it wasn't a priority. My stepfather didn't see me as a quinceañera, my mother couldn't afford it, and my grandmother was surviving and trying to stay afloat. My uncle Raymond was the only one who prioritized that I was a young girl dealing with self-esteem issues. He knew that my friends were having their parties, he wanted me to feel seen like everyone else. So he started to order and store away everything we would need for the big day, from the decorations to platters and serving spoons. He also started a fund to save up for my dress and to rent a ballroom to hold the party.

It was a very exciting time for me. I started telling everybody at school that I was going to have this party, Tommy was going to be my partner. I started picking out my court of guys and gals who were going to dance with us. We started choreographing the dance and just getting ready for the big day. But the more we got into the planning for my party, the deeper Uncle Raymond dove into his addiction. I noticed that he was getting high more often, he was sleeping late, and not going to work on time. But what I didn't notice was that every day, some of the things that he had purchased for my party started to disappear. I was in denial, I wanted to brush past it all because I really wanted that party. It was going to give me status, people would see that I was special too. Tommy and I were going to be quinceañera-official and everyone was going to know it.

When July came around, my uncle was partying a lot. I would come home from work wondering where he was, since he usually met me at the bus stop. But he was secretly hitting the gay clubs in South Beach where he could be around people like him. I was the only person in my family who knew that. I would stay up and wait for him because I was always afraid that something bad was going to happen to him. He was already spiraling. One time, he knocked on our apartment door, and as I opened, he ran straight through and jumped out the back window. The two neighborhood loan sharks had come for him and he had led them to me. When they asked me where my uncle was, I told them I didn't know. They stormed inside our place and searched until they realized he was gone. He had been walking on the dark side for some time but I didn't want to face it because that meant facing that the party, which was coming in a month, was probably not going to happen.

The following night, after the loan sharks, he went out to party again. I remember waiting up for him, I just couldn't sleep knowing he was out there. He called me from the window and I opened the door for him because I knew he was drunk and my stepfather would throw him out if he found out. They knew that I would always wait for him and warned me in advance not to let him in. But I was never going to do that. I let him in and he drunk whispered, "Do you know where that platter is?" My heart sank. He was talking about the serving platter that was going to be used at my party. He was asking me to hand over my last hope—there were no other serving platters left. He searched through the closet and came out holding it up like a trophy. His victory was my loss, I was going to look like a fool at school.

"What are you going to do with this platter?" I asked him, as he walked out the door. "Where are you going?"

"I'll be right back," he replied.

I followed him because I wanted to know what was going on. As I walked out to the front of the building, I saw my uncle attempting to pay a cab driver with the platter. The driver called him a couple of choice words and then surprisingly snatched the platter out of his hands, jumped back in his yellow car, and sped off.

In that moment, nothing mattered to me anymore, not that my uncle was in addiction, that he had just stiffed a cab driver, that he had previously been running from a loan shark. The one thing that sunk in was that I had a boyfriend and it was because he made a way for me to have some normalcy. I knew that he was messed up at the time, but I also remembered all the sacrifices that he made for me. He sold his blood once to feed me. I couldn't help but turn to this because it made me feel better about my life. It was all I knew in dealing with reality. I wasn't going to have my party, but as angry and as hurt as I was in that moment, I remember being washed over in sadness for my uncle, beautiful Uncle Raymond. Living a miserable life where he couldn't be himself, he had reduced himself to trying to pay a cab driver with a Fingerhut platter. And then I remember laughing. I laughed so hard that night because I couldn't believe that he actually got away with it.

The Odd One Out

Once I got back home from that life-altering journey to my roots, I found myself moving further and further away from the DR emotionally. I didn't want to stay in touch with my dad and found myself barely talking to him. It felt like I had gone on an underwhelming date and didn't want to give this guy the wrong impression. We didn't have a future together so I wasn't going to lead him on.

My brother reached out to tell me that my father was complaining to him about me posting more about my Puerto Rico trip than I did my Dominican Republic one. My father didn't like that. Out of all the things to be thinking about, he was concerned with what I was posting on social media. One would think he would be remorseful for his behavior a few weeks back and would now be ready to atone. Nope. He wanted me to validate him publicly. He lived on Facebook and often posted about me. It felt like he was looking for me to assure the world that this American kid was his. I wanted him to show me that I meant something to him, that he loved me. After all the years of wanting him to legitimize me, I had finally figured out that I wanted more. I wanted to be connected and feel secure with him.

With time, my newfound siblings told me that they had endured their own set of challenges with him. We compared stories to see who had it worse. I had the benefit of letting my mind create an imaginary father who could be whatever I wanted him to be. They were faced with who he really was. That couldn't feel good either. We all had sadness around the entire thing. And still they handled him with the utmost reverence and respect, culturally we are programmed to do that. Because sometimes we are just the help, we are not seen as human beings with emotions. We are there to do the work the elders can't do.

Agitated by my lack of communication he started to reach out to them to complain. He kept putting them in the awkward place of asking me to call him. That made me pull away from them also. I stopped responding to messages and taking calls. After all, they were all his family. No matter what happened, they had a lifetime with each other and that had to mean something. They had years together and had to love one another, like family does. I was the odd one out.

I kept it cordial and short, but I was definitely on my way out of this whole situation. Soon I stopped speaking to anyone at all. I suffered daily anxiety thinking about a list of good reasons I should just cut them all out and then I would think about the genuine connection I had with my siblings and nieces and nephews and would feel guilty. I only truly wanted to rid myself of him, but I didn't think that excision alone would be possible. He would always be in the way of my relationship with my siblings. And I believed they would side with him. He actually told me the day after I met him that my mother cheated on him when she was in the Dominican Republic. In fact, he said that he had never been with a woman who didn't cheat. This man was telling me that my teenage mom who was in another country, with no family, sleeping on beaches with her baby took the time to have an affair. Meanwhile, he was almost thirty and he was the one who was sleeping around. He basically set out to demonize my mother, not for taking me away from him, but for being with another man. The entire experience was upsetting because I didn't travel to the Dominican Republic to hear any of this, I went to connect with my father and hopefully begin a new, healthy relationship with him. I didn't want to hear him shitting on women, especially my mother. This guy had a lot of gall talking negatively about the parent that stayed.

After I settled back home, I called my brother and shared with him what had happened at that restaurant in the DR when my father asked me for money in front of my entire production team. My kid brother was so upset that he called my father to confront him. He had asked my father not to ask me for money prior to our meeting. He warned him that it might scare me away—and it did. On July 5, I received a text from my father that hurt more than the proverbial punch in the stomach he gave me in the Dominican Republic. His message was to never call him again, that I wasn't worthy of his time and that God was going to punish me for being a liar. This was just thirteen days after I met him. I was on a trip to Palm Springs celebrating my daughter's birthday. I was still processing, figuring out how I was going to proceed. Even though I kept saying to myself that I was done with him, deep down inside I just wanted him to chase me, apologize, and try to make good of what had happened between us. He broke up with me even though he was the shitty one. This hit hard. I just couldn't believe he had put those words together and shot them at me. Even though he had only given me reasons to believe that he could. I was still learning what it was in me that kept going back for more, looking for the good in others no matter how fucked-up they were.

Out of what I believe to be embarrassment, he denied having asked me for money, basically calling me a liar. That would just add to my entire father-trauma. It made me feel emotionally paralyzed. I couldn't cry or talk, I just curled up on the couch and stared at the wall. He went on my sister's Instagram, the one who lived in upstate New York, someone I had spoken to on the phone once but had never met before, and posted in her comments section that I was innately evil and referred to me as a harpy. I had only read that word in an old book and didn't even know it was still in use. Meanwhile, I was once again left to feel like an outsider, and all he did was continue to pour salt into my wound.

What he didn't know was that the more he wronged me, the more of me he lost. Suddenly, I started to realize that maybe I was better off in life without him. Maybe him not being there was really a blessing in disguise. The father I always wanted in my life was made up in my imagination, somewhere between Johnny Carson and Richard Pryor. It was definitely not him.

Although this all sounds horrible, it is all coming from me and my pain. None of it is made up and it is still my side of the story. All of the things that I learned about my father were from him and those around him. I don't know what happened to him as a child and how he grew up. I am completely unaware of his history and trauma. Even though I grew up poor, I grew up in the States where he continuously fled to seek refuge. I could remain in the place where I made him the villain in my story, but who would that serve? The truth is that he was just as broken as I was, his desperation was just a little louder than mine. I love that man and am grateful for him, he is partially responsible for me being here. I honestly don't know what I am going to do with him. But throwing him away feels petty and vindictive. Giving others grace and forgiving is probably my superpower and not the weakness it has been framed to be. Seeing myself in him is cool and, honestly, the moment he hugged me for the first time, my heart wanted to explode. I met my father, that shit is cool, no matter how rough the ride. Some people never find their dad and I am here trying to figure out what's next with mine. That's privilege.

What's more, I had a village of people who showed up for me in ways that I didn't believe he was capable of doing. The women in my life were strong and loving, they nurtured me so that I was able to receive it. This search for parenting from a man because society told me to now felt like a waste of time. I was looking for answers. I wanted to meet myself. Outside of genetic questions that answered where my anemia came from and trivial curiosities about whether we liked the same music and food, we could've done our meeting over a Zoom. It would have saved me some heartache and time. I really appreciated so much more the sacrifices that came from my tribe: My grandmother used six months of her landlady's pay to take that trip to the Dominican Republic all for me. She sacrificed her trip to her home where she had only one living elderly sister to go find my father for me. It jeopardized our relationship for a couple of hundred dollars while my abuela invested her last cents to make me happy, to help me fulfill this lifelong wish of mine. Turns out, I had what I needed all along, I just couldn't see it because I was too busy hearing the heckling of my third-grade bully. This was the moment I finally put Beth to rest.

My mother, my grandmother, and my uncles, they were my parents.

PART III

W. Wings

Put Some Respect on Akaylah's Name

When my daughter was in kindergarten I would check her backpack daily as a practice, mainly to clean it out, because on any given day you could find anything in there from melted chocolate to a frog. That was my kid. She knew herself. She had a *point of view* at a very young age. If I said that I loved a song, she would remind me that I loved her and *really liked* the song. She wasn't having it, being on the same level as "Say My Name," no matter how great it was. I don't know where she got that from, or if she just finally reached a place where she was able to articulate it.

As I was emptying out the *Blues Clues* backpack, I ran across some of her schoolwork and flipped through page after page of her tracing stencils of letters when I noticed something was off. The name in her heading was spelled wrong, and by wrong I mean that she signed it Akaylah Rodriguez. That was not her last name! I was married to her dad and one of the things that I took most pride in was that she had her father's last name!

The next day I went to her school and had a conversation with her teacher. She was surprised to know that my daughter was writing her name wrong. She assumed that because I was Latina, my daughter was doing what they do in Latin America, which is to use the mother's last name as well. I was really bothered by this, I was rude to the teacher because I felt that she was a bit racist (which, in short, was later confirmed). I told her that we had to address the issue and course correct, I didn't want my daughter going around using my last name as if she didn't have her own. I had actually hyphenated it—as much as I complained about not having my father's last name, I loved Rodriguez more than I was willing to admit.

For the next few weeks, I noticed that the work kept coming home with my last name. I wanted to blame the teacher but if my daughter was refusing to comply, what was she to do? I certainly didn't want her chastising my kid because my daughter was confused about why she and I had different last names. At some point I was going to have that talk with my daughter. I honestly was avoiding it because I had feelings about the situation.

One day after school, I picked up some McDonald's—I was a model parent—and we went back home and sat down to eat as I had planned to have the conversation. This needed to stop. My son, Omar, was also at the school and I didn't want people thinking that I had two kids with different fathers. I had so much shame in life about not having my father's last name and not having the same father as my siblings. All of this was wrapped up in what seemed to be a trigger for me. So after a few nuggets, I turned the Nickelodeon off and dove in. Honestly I had been avoiding it because it was such a touchy subject for me, I unfairly placed this burden on the teacher simply because I did not like her and also because I was a coward. I was so sensitive with how I talked to my daughter because I remembered how easily I was broken by my mother's verbal lashings.

I asked my baby if she knew her name and she looked me in the eye and confidently said, "Yes, I'm Akaylah."

"Do you know your last name? Akaylah what?"

"Akaylah Rodriguez," she said, looking me straight in the eyes and punching me right in the face with it, no hesitation, she knew her name.

I tried to explain last names to her. I thought it was complicated, but it turned out that she knew what they were.

"I want to be Rodriguez like you," she said. "I don't want Daddy's last name."

So many emotions swept through me. I was so confused and at the same time, flattered. She was proud of me and wanted to be like me. She didn't even think about her father, and because he wasn't there, she didn't know him enough to like him, let alone carry his name. The way she saw it, it was a privilege for her to claim me. What a beautiful perception to have at that young age. Damn, she was my hero. I had such shame as a little kid about not having my father's last name, and here she was deleting hers because she didn't deem him fit. Did I do that? Was it me that instilled that sense of self and importance or did she come here with it? Maybe I was just putting more on it than it was. I was simply so honored that my kid felt that way about me, and at the same time, a sense of sadness overcame me because I hadn't felt that way about my mom.

Nonetheless, I decided to let "Akaylah Rodriguez" be. It was something that she needed to express and that was where she was at the time. Her pride overrode my shame, plain and simple. That day when I sat down with my daughter to share a lesson on last names I received one in respect.

Thomas Crown-ish

Let me tell you about the day I picked up the biggest gift anyone ever gave me: a Range Rover. It was custom-made for me. I had never even seen a Range Rover like that; they didn't have those in my neighborhood. In the building where I grew up, there were ten parking spaces in the lot out back. I remember two cars, which were on blocks (one of those was stolen), a station wagon, an '83 Nova, and my mother's Thunderbird. The Thunderbird was yellow with a green spray paint stain on the door, and it was one of the most embarrassing things in my life at the time—and I had many. But that damn car was at the top of the list. My mother would pick me up from school by driving down the main street, honking the horn the entire way, until I just ran and jumped in the car hoping no one had caught sight of me in that car. It didn't matter that we were all poor; you would get so roasted if you jumped in a long, bright yellow Thunderbird with a green stain on the door.

So someone buying me a Range Rover was not only unheard of,

but a nod that I had made it in some kind of crazy way. It was a status symbol and validation of my worth by way of a car, and more important, by way of a man. Girls like me weren't expected to have a Thomas Crown.

My life at the time I received this gift was simple. I was a young single mom who was new to LA, running away from crazy, mainly keeping my kids healthy, safe, and on task. I was fresh out of a divorce and family dysfunction, and I needed to start anew. I moved to LA to pursue my dreams and quite naturally, upon arrival, I did what every actor on the verge of becoming a big star does when they get to LA: I got a day job. Luckily it was at a financial firm and not a restaurant. My hours were nine to five, Monday through Friday, my weekends reserved for trips to Chuck E. Cheese. While my friends were going to parties with rappers and NBA players and doing shots, I was going to school plays and track meets and driving my kids to school in my Toyota Camry with safety pins holding up the ceiling fabric. Many women my age were partying while I was trying to rub gum out of my daughter's hair with peanut butter. I didn't have any help, I had to pay the bills and take care of my kids on my own, so I was constantly worn out. But I was used to doing things for myself. I hadn't depended on anyone since I left home. Nevertheless, life was hard. I had no relatives in LA and didn't have many friends at the time. I remember saying to myself all the time, *Can I just catch a break? Why not me?* Damn, I just wanted to feel like a regular young woman.

Then someone that I respected very much introduced me to this guy. His name was Jax, and he was a sports agent and a very smooth man. There was something very mysterious and charming about him. His swagger made up for that little bear face of his. He looked like a koala (hopefully minus the chlamydia). He was always dressed nice, he had style; whether he wore a suit and designer shoes or jeans and Jordans, he was put-together and I was attracted to that. He had a grown-man vibe, which I was drawn to. Something about a grown-up man made me feel safe and secure.

Jax was into me as well and he let it be known instantly. My low self-esteem could not allow me to understand why. I was exhausted all the time, so I didn't have time for self-care, not much time to do my hair or makeup. I walked around in sweats and a messy bun, while he was dressed in the best, sporting a watch with perpetual motion. The thought that he was better than me because of what he did for a living, because of his financial situation, and because of my low self-perception kept me in a constant state of confusion about why he liked me. But he courted me hard.

The beginning was sweet: flowers and thoughtful gifts. He paid attention. He knew that a single mom probably needed a sitter. So he made it part of the plan and offered to take care of it. I was blown away by this because men didn't usually ask about these things. And to be honest, dating a single mother should come with a rule book. There is so much to know about it and to take into consideration. Everyone can't do it. He could.

Beyoncé came to town, and he got my daughter not one, not two, but *seven* floor seats for the concert. My daughter, her two best friends, her teacher, my two friends, and I all saw Queen Bey at the Staples Center. I don't think you understand: This was the first tour when Beyoncé rode in on a fucking elephant. It was epic! Without meeting my kids, he understood where they were on the priority list. And so, almost seamlessly, he always took them into account. Queen Bey was major points—one of the biggest moments in my little girl's life.

He was making sure that I had a good time too. I am a Detroit Pistons fan, and at that time the Pistons were good. I mean this was Chauncey Billups, Rip Hamilton, Ben Wallace Pistons, the Championship Pistons. Rip Hamilton wore that Tom Cruise *Vanilla Sky* mask and they were on fire. And this man flew me and one of my closest friends first-class to Detroit to see a game. When we arrived, a limo was waiting for us at the airport with a driver named Lady Di. She was different, with extra-long nails and a lace glove on one hand like Prince. I had a white woman named Lady Di driving me around, and it wasn't the bus. It was pure comedy.

Jax met us there after tending to some business with some of his players, and we went shopping. I love shopping. He took me to the mall. He bought my son a new PSP, which was the thing at the time. He would always remember "the children," as he would say. In fact, he told me that he too came from a single mom, so he had a certain respect for me. He took me to Build-A-Bear to buy my daughter a stuffed animal; we built that bear together. *Could this be the daddy for my babies?* I thought. He went on to buy the Build-A-Bear every outfit in the store. We were in a real relationship—that's what a Build-A-Bear means! Single moms can be vulnerable, and I was no different, especially when the father is estranged from the kids. So when a man steps in and says "I see them," it pulls on the heartstrings. I was sincerely moved by the way Jax always included them in the fun and when he talked about the future.

I was raised with conflicting messages as a girl. I was told that women who dated men for money were gold diggers, and at the same time was instructed to find a man with money who could help me get out. I believed that "gold diggers" had to dig because they didn't believe they could get there on their own. This guy believed I *could* get there. "Do you see yourself? You are so close. You just need a little bit of help!" Up until meeting Jax, the only cheerleaders I ever had in my life were my siblings, my grandmother, and my uncles, who were all three thousand miles away. Jax was completely dialed in, thinking about the support I needed as a mom, as a woman, as an artist. He was what my squad and I called a dream pusher, constantly asking me about what I was trying to achieve and how he could help me get there, saying things like "How can I be of service to you?" That was an aphrodisiac if ever there was one.

It felt like I had someone on the team who had my back, and that was impressive, especially because he was still new. It felt like he believed in me. And at this point in my life, I really needed someone to believe in me. I could use the win. I was the belle of the ball for once—yes, me, wearing the pretty dress! It was cool to do fun stuff. The only outings I had prior to meeting him were field trips with the kids and going to Krispy Kreme when the hot sign was on. I was enjoying this, no apologies. All of it: the material stuff, the self-esteem coaching, and everything else that came along with him. But, deep down, I also remember thinking: *Is he a child molester? Does he have an STD? Maybe there is something wrong with his penis, or maybe he has just one ball? His penis can't be that great; men with great penises tend not to be very thoughtful.* Was it too good to be true?

Soon Jax was on the road for a few weeks, working. It was a busy time for him. His clients in college were getting ready for the draft, so he had to travel a lot. I remember getting a call from my friend Sheryl who was a real estate agent. Jax found her on Facebook and contacted her to help find me a house. It was supposed to be a surprise, but of course my fellow Single Mom gave up the info. I was jumping for joy! A house? I had never lived in a house. I grew up in a building in Miami, one with ten apartments, and I lived in seven of those ten apartments. I was raised by a collective of Cuban refugees, undocumented Central Americans, my crazy Mariel boatlift stepfather, and my Puerto Rican feisty mother. The highlight of my days in the building was playing a mean game of kickball with my neighborhood friends. The thought of a house was not only refreshing but a relief, and the car was even more exciting. It was a moving status symbol.

My Range! Jax bought me a Range Rover and had it shipped to me. I was going to pick it up on Friday. I was finally living life, enjoying shit that I had only dreamed of. I cannot lie, my mouth watered at the thought of a black Range Rover with a cherry interior, a full kit, and televisions on the inside. My kids were going to watch their favorite movies while I rode around in style. Everyone was going to know that I was someone, no longer the ghetto chick from Allapattah, Miami.

Friday rolled around, the day to go pick up my car. Jax would not be there, as he was away scouting for a few weeks. The combine was coming up. The plan was that I would pick up the car before I picked up the kids from school. I went and got my nails and hair done; I had to look Range Rover–worthy to go pick it up. I stopped by my girl Ca-Trece's house to grab a handbag. She was a stylist, so she always had shit for us to check out, like a fashion library. I chose a blue Chloé handbag that would pop perfectly with the Range Rover's interior. Between "you fake it till you make it" and "you are what you own," I was drowning in it, a misguided clown, the victim of toxic capitalism, superficiality, materialism, and white supremacy all rolled up in a borrowed and bought-by-someone-else outfit. Everyone in my tribe knew about the car. My friends, my kids, and my mom were all so excited that I would finally have the Range that I always dreamed of. Indeed, years before, I had bet a childhood friend that I would get one before her and now the day had finally come.

During my final ride in my Camry with the safety pins hanging over my head—which I had bought with my hard-earned money but couldn't wait to get rid of—I got a phone call. It was Stacy, the person who introduced me to Jax. He wanted to know if I had picked up the car yet.

"On my way," I said gleefully.

"It's good that you haven't," he said. "You can't pick up that car."

I sped up. I was almost at the finish line, and I wasn't going to let anything stop me. I was almost there, at the next level of *I am somebody*.

"Like hell I can't" was all I kept saying to Stacy. That car was for *me*.

"Pull over!" Stacy shouted.

I paused and stopped the Camry.

"The car is part of a federal investigation and if you pick it up, it will be trouble for you," Stacy said.

"What are you talking about?" I asked, confused.

Stacy explained that Jax had been arrested and that the car was going to be confiscated by the feds. I was completely shaken. I had never been in trouble in my life, never been to jail. But dammit, I wanted that Range. I was willing to fight for it, not stopping for one moment to process that this man was in jail. I figured that he had been arrested for some white-collar crime like tax evasion or money laundering and he would be able to sort it all out. But what about me? I'd have to stay in the same place with the same car holding me to the social status of those on the bottom. I listened to Stacy and took a detour.

That afternoon, I picked up my kids from school in the Camry with a borrowed purse and a broken spirit. But my babies didn't even ask one question about the Range. They were just happy I was on time and there. They never cared about the car, they wanted to know that I was going to be there. They just loved me for me. That was it.

Later in the week, things became clearer. I finally had the strength to call Stacy back, to get the full story. After all, he had introduced me to this man in the first place, and I wanted answers. "A BANK ROBBER, WTF?!" was my reaction. I was dating a Bank Robber! He was robbing banks, Lady Di was the getaway driver, and at times, I was the alibi. I couldn't wrap my head around it at first. He had introduced me to NBA players, he wore custom suits, he was in the mix, people knew him. All the thoughts swirled around in my head. It was like my very own Keyser Söze from *The Usual Suspects*.

Secretly, I hoped we'd get back together. I tried to justify it: yes, he robbed banks, but he gave to the poor. I was poor and he was my very own Robin Hood.

I wrote to him, but he never responded.

I never got the Range Rover, and I never got the house, but Jax did leave me with something. A lesson. I let a guy who hadn't graduated from high school, who scammed many into believing that he was something he was not, who armed himself and robbed more than twenty-five banks trick me into believing that I was special. He set the new standard for how I wanted to be treated, how I should treat myself. I hate to say this, but it's true: he was the best boyfriend I ever had. He conned me into accepting that I could go get the things that I wanted and I didn't need anyone to do it. That I was worthy of a better life, but it didn't make me who I was. The people who mattered were staring at me from the back seat like I was the best thing in the world.

Some people have the one that got away; I have the one that got put away.

Strike

Not too long after relocating to Los Angeles, I took a spin class where I met my friend Tee, who was pregnant at the time. She then introduced me to her friends and I discovered a new group of women who were like me, single moms who were LA transplants interested in artistic ventures, and who also wanted to live and enjoy life. Not like the single moms I saw when I was growing up who seemed older, dowdy, and bitter. The moms I met in LA were bad, in a good way. Beautiful, fashionable, fit, and downright sexy. And immediately I knew that what I was striving for existed, it was around me now.

At this point I had been in two different types of long-term relationships and they both fell into what was, per my estimation, the fuckboy category. That meant men who were dishonest, disloyal, and downright malicious. I was a bit jaded by then and I wasn't looking for anything, I just wanted to tend to my babies, build my career, and have fun with my girls.

Because my friends also had children, we had a system that would always keep our kids together and, we believed, safe. We would hire one sitter and split the bill so that the older kids could keep watch of what was going on and be able to tell us. None of us had family in the city so we formed our own. We'd go to Chuck E. Cheese with our kids and designate a driver, so that while the kids played, we could drink wine and eat pizza and have our own outing simultaneously. Having one another also meant we could go out at night. I love to dance so I would take any chance I got to do that.

The thing about dating as a single mom is that you have so many things to think about. And since I had my own childhood trauma I was extra cautious about who was around. I really had a hard time trusting anyone. I always felt that since their father was so far away, we were vulnerable. One of the things that he prided himself on was protecting us and he really did do that when we were together. He believed in traditional gender roles, so he was the muscle. He was front and center for everything, he would not allow anyone within feet of me.

But things were different now. He was not around and my little girl could not remember that about him. I was protecting my kids. This was new for me. As I was evolving and growing, I still was stuck in some of my old ways. As much as I loved my chosen family of women, I missed having a male presence around to feel safe.

Bowling was one of our favorite things to do, and it was something that we could all do together. Though I was guilty of hogging the basketball game at Chuck E. Cheese and hitting the Skee-Ball, this seemed more appropriate. My kids really enjoyed hanging out with me in a way that made me feel that they enjoyed being with me beyond my role as their mother. We have always had a good time together, I never realized that we had formed this bond. It took others to point it out. And on this night, someone did.

While in a hot and heavy bowling match, we heard a southern drawl ask if they could join the next round. My girl Chrimy was laser-focused on the game, and my kids followed the rule of not talking to strangers, so I was the one left to respond.

"Excuse me?" I said, glancing up and then cranking my neck up farther to look at this six-foot "NBA something tall" man standing in front of me. I thought it was a prank or joke of some sort. "There are plenty of open lanes where you can play," I said. This was definitely not the way to flirt with a person who just bowled a strike. Besides, I had my babies with me, why would you approach us unless you were some weirdo, predator?

"I want to play with you guys. You look like you and your kids are having so much fun." Right as I was thinking about calling security over, this Boss Hog–looking man appeared and interjected, "He's not the smoothest guy, but I think he was trying to find a way to approach you. I'm Bert, his manager, his name is Terry."

Things were even wackier and I was confused. What the fuck was happening? Finally, Terry just went for it.

"Look, I know you are here with your friend and your kids, but I don't know if I am ever going to see you again. Can we stay in touch? I am so sorry, I just realized how this looks. I just wanted to approach you and really didn't know how."

Phew, that was better, because up until that point, I was definitely going to call the law. I can't deny that it was a relief to meet Terry under these circumstances because my book was wide open, right there before his eyes. He knew I had kids, he knew how old they were, so we could skip that part of the conversation. It also once again refuted the notion that I was never going to find a man who wanted me with two kids.

Terry and I began to date soon after. He was in fact an NBA player, all that height was being put to good use. But I felt that this would be too much for my family. My ex-husband, the father of my children, was a former NFL player and I honestly didn't want that life anymore. Nonetheless, we were having a great time hanging out, he helped restore my confidence in dating. He made me feel like a goddess. It was fabulous. After being told that you are damaged goods for so long, you start to believe it. Terry wouldn't hear any of it. He wanted me and made it known. He invited me, a friend, and our kids to a Lakers game and got us floor seats. He spoke to me from the court and later introduced me to his teammates, it was truly such a sweet thing. It was the romance that I needed at the time, one that I never believed existed for someone like me.

Terry was on another page. He was on the fast track to getting married and I was still fighting for my divorce. And I can't lie and say I didn't consider it. He was kind and thoughtful, financially stable, and fine. Still, all I could think about was how I finally got out of the grip of someone who didn't support my dreams. I relocated across the country to go for mine. I had to believe in myself and fight the belief that a man was the solution. Faced with all the messaging I was raised with, I had to take a moment to call myself on the bullshit. Was I really going to get married again and put my individual goals on hold? Can't say I was ready to have another kid; and he didn't have any and wanted some. I never wanted my kids to experience having a stepparent. I said I wouldn't. Although all are not bad, I wasn't willing to risk it. Besides, I still needed time to heal and had lots of inner work to do, that was part of the reason behind my escape. I was reading all the books. And at the moment, I really wasn't interested in anything serious, no matter how much I tried to convince myself of the contrary. So we agreed to kick it. It lasted a few months and eventually we were faced with the inevitable, the breakup. We were headed in different directions—he wanted a kid, and I'd have to re-locate to Texas because he made more money and that was where he lived. It was clear we were not going to work out.

But our departure was loving and sweet. I didn't know it was possible to end a relationship without conflict. This was new to me; it was another level. Growth! I wasn't hearing the phrases that were usually hurled at me during the end of something, the "You're crazy" or the "You have daddy issues," or the "Don't cut me." It was just "This isn't working, but I wish you the best, you really deserve it." In that one statement he earned my respect for a lifetime. There is an entire journal entry about just that one line, it blew my mind.

Breaking News

By the time I had gotten over my short-lived relationship with Terry, I was well into a new life. I was having fun again. Honestly, I was meeting men everywhere, and I still didn't know what I wanted. They weren't all great, but it was a good exercise in learning what I was looking for and what would get me to give you my infamous line, "Let me call you right back." That meant that you were definitely getting ghosted. My girls and me would joke about it all of the time, they knew when they heard those words that it was a wrap.

I was pretty noncommittal at the time, with no thoughts of a relationship. I just wanted to be approached, courted, and wanted. I needed to feel desired, especially after a divorce. I had relationship PTSD and I knew deep down that the only thing I could give a man was a hard time. I was still angry for allowing myself to fall for anyone and hurt from my past relationships, and felt like it was my fault for being weak and needy like my mom and grandmother, so I spent the next three years enticing and running for sport. It became a challenge for some of the men I met—they would get off on trying to land me. I was firm in my stand and I was emotionally unavailable so I never felt any risk in entertaining them. I was playing all the games, my favorite was the "being aloof and they come to you," that was how my friend Brenda described it. I became a master at that one.

But the games get old and you eventually get tired of being alone. At least I did. So I decided to start dating again, I mean actually going out and experiencing things. Up until then, I had been keeping it to phone calls and daytime lunches and nothing more. I decided to stretch. I missed having a good make-out session with someone that I really liked. I wanted more. Then, on one of those odd nights out when I felt that my outfit wasn't right, my hair was messed up, and I could use a little concealer, my friend Layla decided she wanted to stop by an event. She just forgot to mention that the so-called event was a celebrity fundraiser, with plenty of eligible bachelors in attendance. I was in no condition to meet anyone, let alone a man, but I was riding shotgun, so naturally this was a hostage situation. I decided to stay in the car. She said she just had to stop by and say hi as a formality, this organization had sponsored her son's basketball team. I was feeling like I looked like trash and didn't want to be in a social setting. I did not care how long she would take, I would stick it out. I was wearing distressed jeans with a baggy tie-dye shirt and felt like I had put on a lot of colors that day, possibly all of them. There was no way I was going to be seen looking like I belonged in a TLC music video. Naturally, the laws of attraction are real and my friends also think they're funny. Since Layla couldn't get me to step a foot into that ballroom to meet a man, she brought one to me. She actually didn't purposely bring a man to me, she came back with a group of friends, a group made up mainly of men. She knew them since college and they were actually walking her back to her car, making sure she got there safely. Right as she slid into the driver seat one of the gentlemen decided he wanted to know who I was.

"Who's that in your passenger seat?"

"That's my girl A. You met her before."

"I would have remembered if I met her."

To hurry things up, I jumped in, "We haven't met, my name is Aida, and we gotta go." As if that really would work with a six-foot-five Scorpio man who knew he was fine. Enter Rob, the former college basketball player turned coach and educator. He was dreamy, everything I had on my short list: smart, athletic, attractive, charming, and beautiful teeth. As a natural conversationalist, he challenged me from the moment we met. What started out as "we gotta go" became a forty-five-minute conversation with this man hanging on to my every word while looking down at me in the car. We exchanged numbers and I started talking to him that same night until I began to fall asleep on the phone.

I enjoyed talking to him so much that we'd have conversations while I was on the way to pick my kids up from school every day. He was my afternoon ride, better than any playlist. It was so refreshing to talk to someone who had read the books I read, liked the same music, and enjoyed dancing. Damn, this was the guy I didn't know I wanted. We talked so much that it felt like middle school. I talked to him about my dreams and aspirations, my fears and life in general. I always had to feel people out before we started to have the conversation about my kids. He never asked me if I had any, and oddly, that was a relief. I didn't really know who he was outside of these conversations and I was paranoid. I was molested by a man who told people I was his daughter and treated me like royalty outside of showing me his dick. I wanted to make sure that I wasn't talking to a creep that had ulterior motives. We hadn't even gone on a date yet, it seemed almost childish how much we talked without seeing each other. What can I tell you? It was a great departure from my everyday life. I was doing the same thing day in and day out and I was definitely not booking any jobs in the acting world. I worked my day job from home and picked up the kids, made dinner, helped with homework, baths, rinse and repeat. That was life. Rob was the voice of friendship and romance; he was what I looked forward to every day. He was the only person in my world at the time that was only interested in me. I was just a woman. This was the one area in my life where I felt like a human being who mattered. Everywhere else I was a single mom whose sole purpose in life was her children. I completely felt that way but it was nice to just be me if only for a couple of hours a day.

Then we decided to actually meet. I normally would call him on the way to school and then we would pick up at night after my kids' bedtime. But today we were going to meet in person and I was finally going to go out on a date. It had been so long. It was going to be a treat to just leave the house as a woman and wear a pretty dress, and look the opposite of the way I looked the day I met him. I wanted to WOW him. I spent my day thinking about this magical date and I couldn't wait. I was going to wear a red dress that wasn't my usual go-to, but I had just found it at Ross and it hugged my tall and curvy figure in all of the right places. I decided my hair would go up in a ponytail, my favorite hairstyle, and I planned on wearing heels because I already knew he was taller than me, and I really liked that. I just knew this night would be awesome.

I picked up my children and as I headed home the dream guy called me. When I saw his name on the caller ID, I really thought he was going to cancel, but no. He said he missed talking to me that day and had not heard my voice and was just calling to say "hi." I can still remember blushing so hard that I didn't realize my daughter was well into the front seat to tell me that she was hungry. She would do this thing where she would take her seat belt off and put her face directly in mine to make sure she had my attention. She was so damn funny. It was going to be a treat to take her to McDonald's, she loved going there. I didn't answer her. I just headed in that direction and gestured to her to sit back down.

"Who's that?" he asked.

"My little girl."

"Your little girl? You have kids?"

"I have two."

After I said the word *two*, what I heard sounded like a DJ scratching a record. I had to ask him to repeat what he just said.

"When were you going to break the news to me that you had kids?"

I froze, my stomach dropped, and all I could think about was how I had fucked up yet again. My dream guy just referred to my kids as "news" like I was giving him my STD status, like they were a bad thing. I had spent so much time talking to this man without detecting the fuckboy in him and was so mad at myself. It was cool if he wasn't interested in dating someone with kids but to refer to them in that way was not okay at all. Not to me. Even though I had not mentioned them yet, I wasn't hiding them either. I was just enjoying a moment. My daughter did the thing again where she put her face right in front of mine while I was at a stop sign, this time to kiss me. It snapped me out of my dark moment and I was back to making a decision with my six-year-old about what size fries I was going to order. I simply said, "Let me call you right back," and hung up. Then I kissed my daughter back and told her to sit her ass down and put her seat belt on.

The Artist Formerly Known as Daddy

The sense of failure that I felt personally as a mother was so heavy, I made it all my fault that my children didn't have their father because I didn't stay with him. And if only I would've just taken a little bit more time and tried to fix my marriage, my kids would have an ideal family. I just had to allow Baby Daddy to do whatever he wanted so the kids could have their father. I knew that was completely crazy, but I still felt that way. I had been making excuses for the men in my life, starting with my father, for so long that now it was my fault that Baby Daddy didn't want to grow up. I should have raised him better. My daughter deserved to have her father, and because I was uncomfortable, I left. But the reality of it was that he wasn't good for us. At the time, he was very toxic. He was very upset about not being in the NFL anymore, and he wasn't ready to move on. He didn't want to be a parent; he was just there. He was actually too busy trying to chase what he felt he left behind, we became secondary to him. We were in the way, cramping his style. But what was most painful to me was that the children came after me, and I was already in second place. When I left him, he left them, and that made me resent him so much.

When I moved to Los Angeles, I couldn't even talk to him on the phone because it would always end up in a fight. I kept trying to convince him to be the father that I thought he should be for our children. The father I knew he could be. I kept trying to coach him into it. I was flying my children out to see him with my very limited funds because they needed him. After years of placing so much on having a father, I hadn't realized how unhealthy that actually was. And the fact remained that my children were going to be okay with or without him. They had me, they always did. He hadn't really been around—my daughter doesn't really remember him. In a way, for a long time, I needed to be able to say that I was a married woman and that my children's father was in the house because I placed so much importance on that image of the family unit. It was as if my status was elevated because of it. I was willing to have a miserable home and raise my kids in a bad environment for the sake of portraying a "regular" family—it was just sad. It spoke to how much I valued what others thought of me. As I fought to keep my family, I began to understand that roles and rights had been established by a patriarchal social standard that was created to maintain oppressive practices. The more I learned academically, the more I realized it applied to my own life. I came directly from an environment that had its struggles by design, a place of a lower socioeconomic reality.

I began to understand that what I needed in life was to find a healing and wholeness that I could discover for myself. If I did the work, I would continue to find it. I decided to become what I needed to be for my children, an entire person who showed up for them daily, ready and willing to roll up my sleeves and do the work. I wanted to be present and attentive, caring, aware, and nurturing. And above all things, I wanted to provide them with unconditional love and understanding. What they really needed wasn't about motherhood and fatherhood. It was about parenthood. But I didn't know that then. I had to learn it as I continued being committed to growth. I had been told that if you didn't have a father in the home, you were probably destined for failure. Because I had failures in my own life and my father wasn't there, that made sense to me, but everyone has failures, even those with fathers in the homes. So there I was, standing fearful that my children's lives would be a mess because their father wasn't present, without taking into consideration that his presence could have brought more harm than good. He had not made the same commitment as I did. I was in my twenties when I was separated from my husband. I had two babies and I managed to move to another state in search of a new life. I kept asking myself, "How am I going to raise these kids without a father in the home?" And there I was doing it.

The constant feeling of not being able to hold it together, taking full responsibility for everything, was hard. But that was how it was. My cards had been dealt. It was my reality. I couldn't compartmentalize responsibility, that's not how it worked. Believing that it was my job to make sure that this thing worked out because it was important for the children kept me going. I was important too, I couldn't raise healthy people if I wasn't healthy. I was always forsaking myself, my sanity, my peace, my happiness, my dignity, my self-respect for others who had no consideration. My mother, my father, Baby Daddy, and others were all responsible for making me feel like I didn't matter. It was time to face that and to understand that I was raised to believe these things, that this was not the way it was. It was not true. Instead of accepting that, I made a decision that I was going to do everything that I needed to do so that my kids could turn out to be productive, loving, and healthy humans. Having a dad wouldn't guarantee that. So I decided to fully immerse myself in the mission to raise the kids the best way I could. I read all the books about parenting I could. I even read books about fatherhood. I sat down and created a plan for myself and my children and how I was going to handle this going forward. There were budget spreadsheets for time and money. Goals were set for the week, months, and years ahead. I talked to my children about what activities and sports they wanted to participate in. I made financial plans to achieve our goals.

I also made it a point to be present. I was at every football and basketball practice with my son, assisting the coaches, being everything that I could for him in the areas where his interests were. I showed up for my daughter's performances, was there for every single field trip, and read in her class, which was important to her. It had nothing to do with gender roles. It was about being present. Being a parent was easy, being a good one was work. And it was one of the hardest things I ever took on in my life. Anybody who does it should get a medal. Being there for your children and being present in every way, not just providing them with food and shelter and clothes, but being there, being able to sit down for homework, whether you understand it or not, was something that I was about. Because I had this belief that if I showed up, they were going to be fine, and I was right.

The absence of the father of my children in their lives was the beginning of the healing of the absence of my father in mine. I had to learn to give myself credit and grace for where I was in life and all the things that I had accomplished in spite of the past. I reminded myself to write down my accomplishments for the month and celebrate them. This was character building for me. The truth is that I really began to see myself through them because they were balanced and pretty damn awesome. Yes, they had challenges and they also felt the void of not having their father. My son had a football ceremony where the boys on the team gave the moms a flower and the dads a hat. My son was the only kid on the team with no dad, he gave me both and had his entire team bend the knee for me. They felt the abundance of my presence in everything that they did, and that really built them up. That was very healthy for their self-esteem. They both had an individual sense of self. They knew who they were and gave off the best energy. Above all things, they knew that they could count on me, that I was going to be there. I learned so much from them. For so long I had believed that I wasn't a complete person because my father wasn't around, now I know that was totally illogical. I was watching these two human beings whom I was responsible for blossoming and becoming the best human beings before my very own eyes. Was I really going to discredit their full humanity because he wasn't around? Absolutely not. So why would I think that about myself?

The Best, Best Man

I had a small wedding, and by small, I mean it was just me, my groom, and my son. I suspected I was pregnant but wasn't really sure at the time. I was sick as a dog. We didn't have guests for two reasons. One was money. We lived on the West Coast and our entire families were on the East Coast and they couldn't afford to come to a last-minute wedding. The second reason was that this was a marriage we were pressured into. We were constantly being told by my family that having two kids out of wedlock was unacceptable. Even though most of them had their kids with no marriage at all.

I prepared for this wedding as best I could, trying on dresses while taking breaks to throw up. This was one of the moments that I had been waiting on for a very long time—that fairy-tale wedding with the big dress and my very own Prince Charming. As a matter of fact, the very first script I ever wrote, when I was in fourth grade, was about my wedding to Michael Jackson. He was my favorite artist, my first crush, and we were both born on August 29. Before even knowing what the concept of a vision board was, I taped pictures of the things that I wanted in life on my bedroom wall, and he was one of them. I wanted the biggest star in the world to marry me before I even knew what a husband was. In this elaborate wedding, my father would walk me down the aisle beaming with pride and then shed tears as he lifted my veil to confidently hand me over to the man that would take charge and see to it that I had a good life. Later, my father would serenade me at the reception and everyone would know how much he loved me.

None of it happened. I didn't get to wear the big, beautiful princess gown I wanted. The long Vera Wang gown with the train that had detailed beads and a beautiful laced veil. I wore a Jessica McClintock dress. It was a very simple, modest dress that covered me from top to bottom. I was pleasing everyone, my Muslim husband-to-be and my Seventh-day Adventist family. It was off-white, of course: I wasn't a virgin, so pure white was not an option.

I had lost my virginity before getting married and that became the focus of family gossip. As if any of them were ever a virtuous bride. I was to right all the "wrongs" of those who had come before me by hiding it with a marriage. I had that option. My mother and grandmother both got pregnant and didn't marry the fathers of their first child. That was common where I came from. We were poor, many people couldn't afford to go get an education, they had to work to survive. A baby was an easy check, and when you don't believe you can do better, you usually don't. When I got to high school, I had already broken a cycle: I was the first woman in my family to make it beyond middle school.

I was in a chapel in Vegas with my Muslim groom, getting married by a Christian minister. I was having what I believed was the worst morning sickness I could ever imagine. Honestly, I didn't know if it was a pregnancy or my body having a volatile response to this wedding. I wasn't ready to be a wife, I was still getting used to being a mother—my son was three—and I had just left school. Everything happened so fast. I didn't need to get married at that moment.

We fought a lot, we were struggling with so many pressures. My baby daddy/fiancé had been drafted by a professional football team and was fighting for his position. He was dealing with politics and hazing from his teammates. I wanted to go back to school to get my degree. And yet here we were, preparing to walk down the aisle in the midst of absolute chaos.

As we got ready, we realized we had never really thought about how the actual ceremony was going to go. There was no wedding party, no maid of honor, and no best man. It was just the three of us.

When the pastor asked who was going to give me away, before I could have a moment to feel sorry for myself, my three-year-old son Omar raised his hand. He looked so proud to do it. It was as if he knew that it was his job. This baby was a supersmart kid, he began talking when he was one, reading when he was three, and now standing up for his mom at almost four. The wedding was a big event for him because he was with his mom and his dad. He didn't know what any of it really meant but he understood that it was important and he was going to participate.

All the doubt that I was swimming in didn't keep me from walking down that aisle because I saw how happy my son was and I loved his father. We would figure out a way. Omar ushered me down that aisle, smiling ear to ear, beaming, holding my hand. I melted the entire way.

And you know what, I am not with the man anymore, but that little boy grew up to be one of the best human beings on this planet, and he is still right by my side. My baby gave me away and was the best man all at the same time. He stood right next to me while I said "yes" to his father and it was as if all the other stuff had gone out of the window. Nothing made me feel more seen, valued, or loved. It was one of the sweetest moments in my life.

PART IV

Flight

You Can't Handle the Truth

For a large part of my life, I thought that the answer to every problem that I had was finding my father. But when I finally met him, the only thing that I found was more questions. In addition to the basic questions—such as Where have you been? How could you move on without me? Did you remember my birthday or were you thinking about me on Christmas?—I also had more profound questions regarding what it all meant for me now. Where do we go from here? Are you going to make up for not being around and do the right thing? Those questions then became burdens because I really had this idea about what my life was going to be once I found him and I didn't take into account what my life actually was at that moment as well as his reality. I was in a much better financial situation than my father. I lead a life with far more privilege than he and my other siblings. What exactly was he supposed to do now? Support me financially, show up at my big events and cheer? What was the healthy balance in a relationship as an adult with my father, who had not been present for the majority of my life? I honestly don't know—I am still trying to figure that out. I suspect that I will continue to figure this out with time.

The narrative that him being absent was my handicap was something that I actually accepted as the truth. You hear it so much it starts to shape what you think. I remembered when I sat down on the couch in that hotel room in the Dominican Republic the day I met him. Faced with the reality that he probably needed me more in that moment than I needed him, my feelings didn't matter because his general well-being weighed more. I thought about myself and then about how hard it must have been for him.

When he listed off his problems that day, I felt survivor's remorse. I was right back at putting myself last. Like the time my mom shared her molestation story with me while doing my hair and ignored the bruise my teacher left on my head. Or when I was bullied at school but didn't say anything because my grandmother was having her gallbladder removed and I had to focus on translating. I was right back to that feeling of being last. The visit with my father did nothing to make it better, it actually made it worse.

I thought that I was going to be healed, everything was going to be fine after my visit to the Dominican Republic because for years I had built that expectation in my head. I was not willing to face the fact that in addition to my daddy issues, there were a myriad of other things in my life that were not about him, which I needed to face. The reality of my own choices was upon me. If I was to be an evolved, better version of myself, I had to start taking accountability. Blaming him was not enough anymore, especially now that I knew he could do nothing about it.

My whole life I had been surrounded by people who made questionable choices about their lives and couldn't deal. Many of them turned to substance abuse, crime, and anything that would keep them from facing their realities. I was not those people, I knew better. That is what I bragged about, I wasn't like them. So, who was I now that I didn't have an excuse anymore? Now that I was dealing with integrity and transparency, I had to be a grown-up. Years of criticizing the adults in my life for not being adults made me forget that I was one of them now. The children were now watching me, I was the one setting the example. I had to put on my big-girl pants and be real about where I was in my life. I had been stuck. I was the victim in my mind for so long that I forgot the champion that I had become on the ground. I had overcome so much without a father and raised two amazing humans without a father. I didn't give any credit to what I actually had in my life because I was too busy wallowing in self-pity and ungratefulness. It was time for a reset.

It had to start with forgiveness. It began with my stepfather. I had been so angry with him for so long that I never ever thought about him as a person—he had just been the bad guy. Yet multiple things can be true at the same time. And though, yes, he had been problematic and insensitive with me, I couldn't live focusing on that forever. I chose to remember that he ran with me to the hospital when they feared I was suffering an embolism. He would not go to bed unless he made sure I ate. He always loved my children—he would take my son with him everywhere he went and sit and watch TV with my daughter all day, *The Proud Family* was their favorite show. He was growing and evolving too, I just stayed in the past for so long, I didn't take notice. Ultimately forgiving him was about my own healing and that had nothing to do with where he stood.

I also had to hold space for my biological father. This man obviously had a rough run at life and dealt with many hardships of his own. These were generational traumas that we were dealing with, they didn't just magically go away. I will someday be held accountable for my own. It started here, with me, this was the moment.

The Village People

When I was seven years old, I sat in front of my sliding door, waiting for my father to show up. I hadn't spoken to him, never had any type of interaction with him after we left the DR. But for some reason, I believed that he would appear that night. My mom kept telling me to go to bed because I had school the next day. This was an act of rebellion for me just as much as it was of faith. I sat on the couch waiting for my father, looking at the trees, asking the trees if he was going to show up. They were shaking and that meant yes. That was the beginning of me believing in them. From that moment forward I would rely on the universe to confirm my beliefs. The trees would answer my questions, the animals would show me signs of what was to happen. I counted on stars for directions. I had been raised with religious beliefs that were specific to Christianity alone. The notion that magic was evil when the Bible was filled with it didn't compute for me. I kept looking to the squirrels for answers, that worked for me.

He didn't show up that night. But I still decided to believe in magic. It was part of a system of values that I was developing to guide me in how I was going to live my life. I believed in the impossible. I needed something other than what my family taught me. I didn't trust it, so much had happened to me on their watch. The disappointment that came with wondering where my father was and if he would ever show up was a driving force in me taking matters into my own hands. I was in charge now and my way was going to work.

Later in life, after years of my dad not showing up, I accepted that it probably wasn't going to happen. I had other goals. As a young girl, I had always gravitated to the arts, even though I was told repeatedly that it wasn't practical or realistic. But I was still in love with the idea of expressing everything I was feeling through entertaining. I was in love with the idea of performing, so I pursued that dream. I wrote my first play when I was thirteen. I wanted to be just like my heroes Lucille Ball, Irene Cara, and Richard Pryor. I actually shut out the noise from everyone around me telling me that I needed to be a lawyer or a teacher and kept that fire and desire burning inside of me to myself. My grandmother had always told me to keep one secret to myself. I decided this was the one because no one around would ever understand or encourage me. I knew that my father was a singer in a band, so I always felt that if I ever met him that would be one of the places where we could relate to one another. But until then, I had to be the wind beneath my own wings.

I decided that I was going to become an actress. I wanted to be a star. That night that I waited for my dad was fuel. That was the day I started to tell myself that I could be anything I wanted to be. I remember being angry and bold. I was a kid, but I knew what I wanted. That night, as I waited for my dad to come get me, my uncle Raymond showed up. He had been in the neighborhood and decided to stop by. Uncle Raymond was my favorite person in the universe, he was a beautiful human being, inside and out. I believe that he saw me staring through the glass door and decided to come upstairs to our place because he didn't want me to feel alone. He would often do stuff like that, that's just who he was, a kind soul. My mom heard his voice and came to check up on me to make sure I was okay. She thought something weird was going on because I was just sitting on the couch gazing out the glass doors. I was waiting for a vehicle to show up and for my father to pop out. It was a real moment for me, I didn't know how it was going to happen, I just knew that it was. When it didn't, I actually didn't feel as bad as I thought I would. My uncle filled every moment of the evening with joy and laughter. He was there to remind me that what I needed was right in front of me. Someone who knew me, who had been around my entire life, and showed up for me as much as they could. We just sat on the couch and watched television and laughed. We watched *The Mary Tyler Moore Show* and I remember thinking to myself that my uncle really loved me.

They say that history repeats itself. I remember this exact moment in my daughter's life. It was about a year after her father and I split. She sat on the steps in my apartment to wait for her dad. I was with John. John and I had been in a relationship now for several months. We were all getting ready to go out and as I attempted to put her shoes on, she started crying because she did not want John to be around. She wanted her daddy. She was four and knew things were changing. She wasn't ready to accept it. So she just sat down on the steps, wearing jeans that were long enough for her, I made sure of that. She begged me to send John away. She just said, "I want my daddy. He is going to come." I sent John home and had to become her Uncle Raymond in that moment.

That was when I realized that now my daughter was in the cycle that I had been in, and there was no way that I was going to allow that to happen. I sat down on the floor next to her and I put her shoes on. I picked her up and gave her a real big hug. I kissed her on the forehead and all over her face, that made her giggle. I was not going to let my baby girl waste time waiting for someone who wouldn't bother to show up. We went out, just the three of us. We got some pancakes and then I took them to see the Shrek movie. I wanted to make sure that she felt seen, that she understood that her life was full, and that she did not have a handicap.

I thought I had done it differently, my daughter was born out of a marriage. I did it the right way, and it still turned out the same. Her father was not ready to be a father, and there was nothing I could do to force him to be. I had to push forward being the best mother I could be while encouraging my children to be their best selves. Sometimes your father isn't there, sometimes your father dies, are you not going to be a complete human being because of his absence? Absolutely not, that was not an option! This was the daughter that my husband wanted and asked for. I bargained with him and brokered off my college education because I wanted to please this man. I thought this baby was going to fix our marriage. "This one is a pistol!" That's what the doctor said when she was born, and I believed him. She was going to be strong and relentless. And so I leaned into that, and I continued to pour into her. She was not going to be broken because her father was not around, neither of them was going to be.

I had believed for so long that having a dad was such an important part of your growth and development, that I counted out the possibility of a great life without one. I had put so much weight there that I kept forsaking myself on all that I was doing. I really believed that this man's mere presence in the home would be enough to affect the trajectory of my kids. I projected so much of that onto my children, so many of my fears and insecurities, so much of my pain, that I would commiserate with them when their father wasn't around. I made a pact to never speak negatively about Baby Daddy around them because I didn't want that to affect their self-esteem. But I also contributed to the fantasy and the romantic notion that he wasn't around because of the injustices that life handed him. I was enabling him.

And so when my kids were four and eight, I remember making the conscious choice to start informing myself. I read self-help books like Napoleon Hill's *Think and Grow Rich*, and Joseph Murphy's *The Power of Your Subconscious Mind*. I took to text about metaphysical thinking, I even read *The Secret*. Those books started really informing me as a young mother about the power of my thinking. Connecting with that moment of discovery when I was seven years old waiting for my own dad on that couch. The magic that I spoke of was really understanding how my subconscious mind worked. I started to believe that I could achieve and obtain what I wanted like I had proclaimed when I was little. None of the circumstances in my life would determine where I was headed, that was my decision.

I was a good kid. I was a great student. I lent a hand at home, I was my grandmother's helper and translator. I took care of my great-grandfather when he was sick. I cared for my siblings. I was a good big sister. I was a good kid in my community, so much so that I had been up for an award for starting an anti-drug organization at the age of fourteen. It was a tribute to my uncle Carlos, whom we lost to drug abuse. And I did all of that and more with a mother, grandmother, great-grandfather, and five uncles. I never stopped to take inventory because I was too busy believing that I was low on stock. I never really understood how instrumental those around me were in shaping me into the person that I had become. I took everyone else who did show up for me for granted because society told me that they weren't enough. Yet I was that little girl crossing the street in Miami, whose grandmother poked her head out of the window to make sure I got to the other side of the street. I was the little girl who had five uncles who showed up at every turn. I was the little girl who had a great-grandfather who would make his famous white rice with red beans, and would have them waiting for me on every Sunday. I was the little girl who had a mom who would walk to school to feed me to make sure I ate. I was the girl whose grown-up friend would shoplift school clothes for me so that I would have pants long enough for my body. I was the girl who had Ms. Rolle tell me that I could be anything I wanted to be and I believed her. I was having a full and complete life experience, but I didn't realize it because I kept being told that something was missing. It wasn't, that was a lie. Even later, when I was raising my own children and an amazing community of people showed up for me as well, I still believed that my missing parent was the key to everything when everything was right before my very own eyes. Many people have a missing parent and feel the void. It is valid, and it is real, and I understand the depths of the pain and the questions. But there are many people who have done great things in life despite the losses. I now refuse to let anyone dictate what makes me complete and my family valid. My life was and is complete.

One of my favorite sayings is "It takes a village to raise a child." I don't recall anyone ever saying what the village looked like. Turns out the village can be many things. And even though my village sometimes looked less than ideal to others, it was where I came from, and it was perfect for me!

Davie

My grandmother has always been proud that I have her name, she loved to tell people that I was named after her. I had a nameplate to prove it, just like her. That necklace was precious to me, I wore it everywhere proudly. In addition to being on trend, it was paying tribute to one of my favorite people on the planet. Children wearing jewelry in Miami was very popular, everything from azabaches (onyx stone), to block the envious eyes, to the saints that protect us. Necklaces and bracelets, we were dripped in gold. While this was happening in the 1980s, a crack epidemic was making the crime rate skyrocket.

I was in seventh grade summer school, and it was one of those superhot and muggy Julys in Miami. I had had the longest day, and I was tired and hungry and couldn't wait to board the bus and go home. The walk from the entrance of the school to the bus was more like a trek and I felt a complete mess. My shirt had a stain on it, I was all teenage sweaty, and I had homework from every class, which meant I was carrying six heavy-ass books. One of my classmates stopped me to ask a question about class and as I grabbed my notes from my jumbled backpack, I felt an aggressive tug on my neck. A guy on a bike snatched my chain and casually rode off as if he hadn't just committed a crime. I was devastated. He took my nameplate and I was going to get in trouble because my mother told me not to wear it to school and I did anyway. It made me feel cool and not so poor. But I had no time to cry. If I missed my bus, that would make it all worse. As I ran over to the bus, I heard a ruckus among a group of people, which usually meant a fight, but I couldn't quite see. The crowd blocked my bus, which was a relief because I was able to slow down a little as I struggled to get on and find a seat. After I sat down by a window toward the back, I heard someone say, "Aidita." I stood up and looked out the window wondering if anyone was calling me at all. As the crowd dispersed, I saw my uncle Davie holding my chain in his hand and the guy who took it hustling to get back on his bike and get away. My uncle saw what happened. He would come to the school to check on me and had some of the older kids keep an eye on me. I never knew that. There he was standing the victor of the fight with my name dangling from his hand, smiling through a bleeding lip. We looked at each other and laughed, realizing that watching all those Bruce Lee movies had finally paid off.

Uncle Davie gave me the gift of comedy in many forms. I learned about stand-up watching it with him. He also unknowingly taught me how to turn our lives into funny. He would always laugh at the uncomfortable and people in our neighborhood would call him crazy. I would beg to differ; I think he was the sanest of them all. He learned to process his traumas through the lens of humor and survived. He could diffuse any situation to buy him enough time to run. He was and will always be my childhood best friend and there is no more joy for me than to invite my uncle, who is highly decorated in his Puerto Rican flag, up on stage for the world to see. He is one of the best humans ever and now I'll fight you if you disagree.

Name Dropping

In the comedy world there is a saying: To get good, you go on the road; to get great, you go to New York; and to get famous, you go to Los Angeles.

It all started with a simple brunch. My friend Leah was having her birthday party and she asked me if I would roast her. It was 2007 and roasts were popular in comedy, everyone was doing them. Leah was a comedy lover, we usually met up on Sundays at the Laugh Factory for the *Chocolate Sundaes* show. It showcased some of the funniest people in comedy and shined a light on comedians of color who would get overlooked in other spaces. This was the hottest room in LA at the time, it was hosted by a brilliant comedian named David Arnold.

I said yes to the roast. I had already been attempting to write jokes at my day job with my co-worker Eve, who happened to be a comedian too. She gave me notes and taught me some of the basics about writing a bit. My love for comedy was strong. It was a new romance that was in the air for me. I didn't think I would actually do it, but I dreamed I would. On the day of Leah's brunch, I sat nervously at my table going over what I had written, mired with second thoughts. I wasn't sure that I could pull it off. Then, while my cold feet were settling in, a well-known comedian named Chris Spencer walked in and sat with us. Leah and I both knew Chris for many years, she had gone to school with him and I knew him from my ex's football network. While I was in San Diego one of my jobs was being an events coordinator. I hosted celebrity basketball games and golf tournaments. Chris would come down from Los Angeles to play in them. We had been friends since then, but honestly, we didn't know what to expect. This was no comedy audience; this was a birthday party.

Leah's mom spoke first and then it was my turn. First one up. I was the rookie, that's how it worked. When I touched the podium, I was petrified. It was weird because I had always been funny to my friends and never felt any fear when I was making them laugh. This was exactly why Leah had asked me to do this. This was different, the laughs were expected. So, I settled into my spot, took a deep breath, and after my first joke got a laugh, permission was granted to deliver another, and another . . . until it was over. The room roared and I couldn't believe the amazing response. I sat down back at the table relieved that it was over but quietly ecstatic that it went well. Afterward, Chris told me that he believed I was a natural and that I should at least give it a try. He had been in comedy long enough to be able to spot a comic. He gave me the name of an open mic called The Westwood Brewing Company, which was by the UCLA campus, and I stashed it away for the time being.

Weeks had gone by and that open mic was the last thing on my mind. I had just ended a six-year relationship and had sworn off men for the time being. I had also lost my job and my car, my ex-husband was not helping, and my kids needed me. I was homeless, everything that I had worked for was now gone. I went from sleeping in my car and Best Westerns with homeless vouchers to staying with my friends who opened their homes to me. Melanie, Rodney, Carmen, Ca-Trece,

April, and Vanessa gave me a place to live, but more important, a family away from home. I don't know what it was on this particular night, but I decided to take Chris up on his challenge and I headed to the open mic with my friend Melanie. I was going to try it no matter how scared it made me feel.

When I reached the spot, I quickly recognized some comedians who I had seen on television. They actually knew what they were doing and here I was pretending, but I did it anyway. That was my first day, and I haven't stopped since then.

Stand-up comedy gave me the voice that I never thought I had. After spending my life searching for validation, it became the place where I found it. It has been a relationship that I have been willing to fight for because it actually gave back. My entire life my goal had been to go back and save the child in me, the little girl who was not proud of her name and felt less than because she didn't have her father. Here I was stepping up to a microphone about to give a sound to all those feelings and power to the shaking voice behind them.

My very first show was an actual paid opportunity that came from a comedian named Speedy who invited me to be on his radio show on the Jamie Foxx network, The Foxxhole. I had no idea what I was doing, I was completely oblivious to the process of comedy. I thought that you just walked on a stage and said whatever was necessary to get a laugh. That is exactly what I did and I actually pulled it off. The audience laughed and clapped and I still had no clue what I had just done. Then they flew me to Phoenix with Bern Nadette Stanis, Thelma from *Good Times*, whom I thought was one of the most beautiful people on television growing up. This was big-time, I got paid five hundred dollars and felt like I had cheated them.

The following week, I went to *Chocolate Sundaes* and felt emboldened from what had happened in Arizona, which meant I took for granted that this was a different setting, a church setting versus a real comedy audience. I had to be ready for this. Leah asked the promoter of the night, Pookey Wigington, if I could do the First Impressions show. This was a three-minute introductory spot for newer comedians to get showcased in front of the audience. I didn't have three minutes, but the show I did the weekend before fooled me into believing I did. Pookey was reluctant, he felt that I wasn't ready. He was trying to save me from myself. He had been in the game long enough to know who was and wasn't ready. But I was arrogant and loud and had grown used to my common humor carrying me through. Yet this was not a dinner table, this was a full house at the Laugh Factory. I hit that stage with all the confidence in the world. My first minute got laughs, I was actually doing some of the jokes I had written with Eve. And then the laughs tricked me into believing that I could just coast. As I ranted about nothing, the audience went completely silent. That happens, but professional comedians know how to deal when it does. I didn't, I felt my stomach drop and the lights get hotter. Audience members stared at me with a mix of disdain, pity, and secondhand embarrassment. I wanted to die—I did, on stage. It was over before I knew it and I just became material for the host of the show. When I got back to the table, Leah and my friends consoled me. That was the night I decided I wanted to be a stand-up comedian. I wanted to figure it out and conquer it. It was exhilarating knowing that everyone was listening to me. Just me. I had to figure this out.

I had a full-time job and going to the open mics at night was my therapy. I kept doing it but I never really thought it was going to be a career. There was no money in it. I did it because it was cathartic, I did it because I loved it. I started to write about my personal life and it was freeing. I was sharing a part of myself that had been locked away. I felt power in telling my stories. I was developing my voice. A year and a half after I started, my friend Vanessa, also a comedian, got me on a military tour with her and several other women. We performed for two weeks in South Korea in several bases. I had never been to Asia and I hadn't been paid for comedy since Arizona. It was a life-changing experience. They had all been doing comedy longer than me, so I learned a lot from just watching them in action. My confidence was growing, I was getting in practice. After that, I kept doing stand-up for several years, it remained my favorite hobby. As for my personal life, I was finally back in my own place, still working full-time, and things were looking up.

In the summer of 2013, I got a call from my manager—yes, I had a manager now—telling me that they wanted me to come in for *Last Comic Standing* on NBC, which was now being produced by Wanda Sykes and Page Hurwitz. They were focusing on creating a more inclusive show that highlighted gifted voices in comedy. This was a big deal, *Last Comic Standing* had been successful and created a pathway for many other comedians who were doing big things. I didn't really think I would get on, but I wanted to give it a try. I needed a boost in my career, and this could definitely help me get some more work and elevate me to headlining status. I was already featuring for Russell Peters, Faizon Love, and Corey Holcomb, but I wasn't making enough money for comedy to be my career. Thankfully, these guys each gave me extra money because they knew that what the clubs were paying was not enough. I decided to do the audition and forget about it when I was done. "Leave it at the door" was my mantra. I went on with my life.

On August 10, 2013, I lost my grandmother to cancer. She had been fighting it since 2000 and I honestly didn't think she would succumb to the disease. She was the strongest woman I knew, my personal hero. I was getting ready for a show at the Hollywood Improv the night she died, and I just crumbled to the floor. I had no idea how to find the funny in that moment, I just cried myself to sleep. It was one of the worst days of my life. Two months after her passing, my uncle Raymond was beaten in a hate crime in Miami and died two weeks later. Two of the most important people in my life were taken in two months and I didn't know what to do. I had not experienced this type of loss since I lost my uncle Carlos and my great-grandfather as a kid. I was in California, away from everyone, and I didn't get to say goodbye. Devastation set in as my heart broke into a million pieces. I had to get on with life because I had a family to take care of, but simply getting out of bed every morning was an enormous feat.

Amid this pain and heartbreak, in the fall of 2013, my manager,

David, called me and told me that I made it to the next round of the show. I couldn't believe it. It was the hardest thing I ever had to do in comedy. Trying to find the funny while grieving seemed impossible. I felt guilty for even making the attempt. I had to work through my pain and really push myself.

On the first show we taped, I wore a yellow dress to honor my grandmother—it was her favorite color—and accented it with my uncle's church deacon pin (he was so proud of his deacon status at Bethany SDA). She always told me to show up for big events looking my best. I clearly remember the joy she radiated each time she saw me in the elaborate dresses she bought me when I was a little girl. Honestly, it made me love wearing them too. I took them both with me on stage that night and I believe they were the ones who gave me the strength to make it through my set.

Roseanne Barr got me right away. Keenan Ivory Wayans pointed out to be careful not to let wardrobe become a distraction, but he gave me the nod to move forward to the semifinals. This was the moment in my career when I had some decisions to make. Who was I going to be in comedy and how was I going to show up? That night I made a choice. I was going to continue to dress up. It was who I was and there would be no apologies. I had been wearing loud dresses with shiny shoes since I could walk. My grandmother would be beaming with pride, and that meant the world to me. I was finding my own way and being my own person in this thing and it ended up paying off because I made it to the top ten. I was a finalist. That changed my life. I was able to quit my job and focus on comedy full-time because it was paying off in more than laughs.

As I hit the road, more opportunities came my way. Tamra Goins and Valarie Benning booked me on the Shaq All Star Comedy Jam tour and I earned a spot on the final season of the Showtime series. A producer named Edwin Licona booked the third season of *Entre Nos* on HBO and I became the first woman to headline one of the installments. It was the first time I felt seen and validated by my community.

During this time I had been working nonstop, I had ended a

relationship with one of the kindest souls on the planet. I eventually broke it off with him because he was younger, and I didn't want to stand in the way of him having children. My kids were young adults and on their way, and I didn't want to have any more children. I vowed that I would never have children from different men—my kids would never know that life. And so, I was finally able to focus on me and what I wanted, and was ready to plunge forward.

I later began to date someone who was older than me, also had grown-up children, and wanted similar things in life. He was supportive, kind, and a very loving father. He even daddy'd me and I loved it. I was still craving that thing that I always thought I wanted. It was the first time I lived with a man who wasn't my husband. We were managing young adult children while trying to maintain careers. I was working and building my path, and he supported me. He knew how much I had put into my career.

Then my friend Tiffany Haddish called me with an opportunity and paycheck of a lifetime. This love affair with comedy was now exclusive. Tiffany had told me that she was going to produce my special but I didn't think that it would happen so soon. She had recently taken off and was busier than ever. But she did it. She took a pay cut so that six comedians whose specials she was producing could get paid a decent wage. She joined forces with Page Hurwitz and Wanda Sykes and produced the *They Ready* series that was wildly successful. That show was the very first time I opened up about my journey with my father in a real way. It was me at my boldest, speaking my name proudly, incorporating it into my act. I had come full circle, again. Then, my agent at the time, Tasha Brown, was able to negotiate my one-hour comedy special deal for me with HBO Max, which aired in 2021. A group of several women assembled themselves along the way to push me to my next level, which eventually led me to this very moment. And now, here I am, writing the last words of my very first book where I teamed up with little me to share my story of finding triumph in words, victory in laughter, and love through it all. How legitimate is that?

ACKNOWLEDGMENTS

Carlie, Benjamin, Emma, Aaron, and Aidan, Tía loves you forever!

Tía Hilda, thank you for being a second mother to me, for showing unconditional love, and always another way. I appreciate you immensely. Carrie and Tiger, thank you for the attention and tenderness you gave. I needed it.

Carlos, Christopher, Damien, Maggie, Elijah, Nicholas, Raquel and Ralphie, Lito and Jackie, and Deondre . . . they call you cousins, I call you extended siblings. Love you.

And to my father, Maximo, and my Dominican family, Tiffany, Mariana, Gandari, Laksmi, Krisna, Tía Isabel, Aida, Laura, Pedro, Leury, Johsly, Jasmine, Azul, Jael, Axel, and Johnathan, though I haven't been around the entire time, the love is real. Thank you for being patient with me.

Orlando, Norma, Ivan, Martika, and Anita. Los quiero.

My chosen family, Elora, Delvis, Auntie Lisa and the Lake family, Diann, Stephanie, Melanie, Ceci, Kibi, Rodney, Carmen, Tiqua, April, Leah, Tiffany, Brady, Tavia, Ca-Trece, Brad, Wendi, Ruben, Chaunte, Courtney, Emanuel, Tish, Artelia, Bryan, Anthony, Orlando, Vanessa, Ramon, Gadiel, Andee, Emory, Carola, Julie, Gail, Gita, Candy, Kwanza, Raleigh, Uncle Fred, Uncle Love, Rochad, Sauce, Jeff, Russell, Marcella, Monica, Marcus, David H., and Carmen. You are all appreciated, thank you for every effort to make my life better.

The Village Kids, what an incredible gift. Ariel, Ashley, Aliyah, Alexis B., Zavien, Sommer, Brad Jr., Charli, Keenan, Louis, Kylah, Sidney, Xavier, Quincy, Alexis W., Alexis OJ, Malik, Jordan, Jaia, Eshe,

Vadim, Nathan, Freedom, Cole, RJ, Ariana, Charence and Sequoia, Teryn and Tenille.

The indescribable tribe, I am EVERYTHING I am because you love me. Till the wheels fall off.

I want to thank Edward Benitez for seeing the book in me and then seeing it through. I am grateful that you understood the importance of my story. Rakesh Satyal, I appreciate your guidance and tenderness through this process of revisiting my past and always showing up on Zoom with a smile. Grateful to Ryan Amato, for being so thoughtful in the process. Cecilia Molinari, you came through and showed up; you know me, you really do. Judith, Melinda, Lucile, and everyone at the HarperOne team who has come aboard to see this win for me.

Ariana DeBose: Thank you for your beautiful words, they were the inspiration that I needed to keep going. To be seen, in that way, by you . . . is the greatest compliment.

John Leguizamo: Humbled to say the least, you are one of the reasons why I do what I do. Master storyteller, fearless, and relentless. Thank you.

Julissa Arce Raya: I can't believe I know you, you are the writer that we all aspire to be. Thank you for reminding me that purpose is instrumental in this thing we call art.

Ben Crump: Who better than you to cosign for me. You have been a witness to my growth and evolution. Thank you for always being that leader and friend.

Marie Arana: What a compliment for you to hold my heart in your hands, thank you!

Jeff Cohen and the Cohen & Gardner family: I know that I am never alone so long as you are here. Thank you!

D.C. Wade: Thank you for rolling up your sleeves and jumping in, it is a true testament to your belief in me. I appreciate you.

Pam Loshak: Thank you for coming aboard and making a difference.

One time for the educators in my life, those who reminded us that we were something special when our environment shouted otherwise: Sylvia Rolle, Eunice Davis, Richard Harris, Mrs. Carter,

Mrs. Flannagan, Sra. Yero, Sra. Castellano, Kris Kirchner, and every single one of you who showed up, forever in your debt.

And then there were whispers of doubt that made me feel that I couldn't do this, but louder than those whispers were Chloe and Yahdon's screams, "Yes you can." Grateful.

ABOUT THE AUTHOR

Aida Rodriguez is a comedian, writer, and actor—a favorite of critics and fans alike. *Esquire* magazine declared of her, "This is Rodriguez's genius—using comedy to turn pain into progress, to give voice to the voiceless, and to laugh instead of cry." Aida's comedy special *Fighting Words* is streaming on HBO Max. She is a key collaborator on the platform's *Entre Nos* franchise, which features the brightest up-and-coming Latinx comedy talent. Aida was not only a breakout star of the series early in her career, she also recently stepped behind the camera to direct its current batch of specials. She is a guest writer for BuzzFeed and Oprah Daily as well as a regular commentator on *The Young Turks*.